ALCHEMY OF THE

MORTAR & PESTLE

THE CULINARY LIBRARY

VOLUME 1

D. & P. GRAMP

ISBN: 1451507119
ISBN 13: 9781451507119

ABOUT THE AUTHORS

Di Gramp trained in the Culinary Arts at both Elizabeth Russells
School of French Cookery and The Cordon Bleu, London,
subsequently working as a professional chef in Mayfair and
as a food lecturer, chef, published writer and Psychologist in
Australia. After completing tertiary studies in visual arts, Prue
Gramp launched a successful Artisan Tea business, studied
food photography and cheese making. The authors co-founded
TheCulinaryLibrary.com food blog in 2011.

Cover image, vintage botanical illustration of the Toothed Wild
Onion, Jacob Sturm (1771-1848)

CONTENTS

INTRODUCTION vii
The Culinary Library—Man's Earliest Culinary Tool—Purpose—
Materials—The Seven Alchemical Stages in Creating Flavor—The
Missing Eighth Alchemical Secret—Choosing the Path of the
Apprentice

HISTORY.. 1
Prehistoric Man—The Indian Book of Veda—The Chinese Yellow
Emperor's Book of Internal Medicine—The Egyptian Ebers
Papyrus—Mexican Aztecs—Old Testament and Biblical Times—
Ancient Romans—American Indians—European and English
Apothecaries—Asia—Russia—Middle East

SELECTION 11
Size Matters—Materials—Cost—Cultural Differences

RECIPES... 17
SAUCES 18
Aioli—Almond—Anchovy—Aubergine—Berry—Bread —
Butterscotch—Coconut Coriander—Creamy Sorrel—Garlic—
Garlic Rosemary—Garlic Walnut—Green 1—Green 2—Honey
Soy—Horseradish—Lemon—Pad Thai—Parsley—Peanut—

Pesto—Pistachio—Plum—Pomegranate—Prawn/Shrimp Cocktail—Roux—Saffron Cream—Sweet and Sour—Tahini— Tarragon—Tartare—Walnut—Walnut Vinaigrette

CURRIES, SPICES, AND PASTES 33
Almond Paste—Chili Paste—Date and Orange Blossom Paste— Dukkah Spice—Egg Yolk Paste—Guacamole—Harissa—Herb Salts—Hummus--Marzipan—Massaman Curry Paste—Moroccan Nut Paste (Amlou)—Olive Paste (Tapenade)—Olive and Caper Paste—Olive and Date Paste—Picada—Pistou—Praline Paste— Quenelle Paste—Ras el Hanout Spice—Rempah—Rillette—Saffron Paste—Sambal Paste—Thai Green Curry—Thai Red Curry—Thai Yellow Curry— Walnut Sauce —Zaatar Spice Mix

MARINADES 49
Aussie BBQ—Balsamic—Basic Wine—Butter Chicken—Carpaccio Beef—Carpaccio Swordfish, Tuna, or Scallop—Chinese—Chicken Tikka—Chinese—Cuban—Egyptian—Fish 1—Fish 2—Garlic Prawns—Lamb—Mountain Pepper—Moroccan—Papaya— Pineapple 1—Pineapple 2—Pomegranate—Sparerib—Spicy Plum—Steak—Teriyaki—Thai

COMPOUND BUTTERS 59
Butter Types Available—Almond—Anchovy—Black Garlic—Blue Cheese or Roquefort—Café de Paris—Caper Tarragon—Caviar— Champagne—Chardonnay and Sage—Chili Lime—Chocolate Hazelnut—Chocolate Orange Jaffa— Chocolate White— Cranberry Sage—Crepes Suzette—Curry Orange—Egg Yolk—Fig Orange—Garlic—Green Tea Matcha—Herb— Honey—Honey Orange—Honey Pecan—Horseradish—Key

Lime—Lavender—Lemon Dill—Lemon Mustard—Liqueur
Cherry—Maitre D'Hotel—Maple Syrup—Montpellier—
Mushroom—Nut—Orange Mint—Pecan Maple—Pesto—Pina
Colada—Pine Nut—Pomegranate Orange—Printanier for
Soups— Red Wine—Roux—Saffron—Sauterne—Smoked
Paprika—Snail— Sour Cherry—Spiced Rum and Raisin—
Tarragon—Truffle— Tuscan Herb—Walnut—Walnut
Raisin—Wasabi—Whiskey

AETHEROLEA 75
Definition—Oils Ain't Just Oils—Technique—Uses and
Types—The Family of Edible Oils: Almond—Argan—Avocado—
Canola—Cottonseed—Coconut—Corn—Colza—Flaxseed—Grape
Seed—Hazelnut—Macadamia—Marula—Mongongo—Mustard
Seed—Olive—Palm—Peanut—Pecan—Perilla—Pine Nut—
Pistachio—Pomegranate Seed—Poppy Seed—Pumpkin
Seed—Rape Seed—Rice Bran—Safflower—Sesame—Soybean—
Sunflower—Walnut—Watermelon Seed. Suggested Plant Infusers.

POTIONS, LOTIONS, AND ELIXIRS...95
Definition—Benedictine—Bitters—Scottish Bitters—Chartreuse,
Green and Yellow—Cold and Flu—Dandruff—Elixir of Youth—
Golden Silk—Limoncello—Liver Potion—Love Potion 1—Love
Potion 2—Miracle Skin Lotion—Rose Lotion—Salvation Elixir—
Show Wu Chinese Energy Tonic—Vital Life

POULTICES 103
Definition—Preparation—Recipes: Bran—Bread—Cabbage—
Carrot—Clay—Green Tea—Jack and Jill Poultice—Mustard—
Onion—Pomegranate—Potato—Plantain—Pumpkin—Walnut

UNGUENTS 109

Definition—Althea—Apostles Unguent—Balm of Gilead —
Basilicum—Black Drawing Salve—Black Walnut Salve—
Camphorium—Chest Congestion Salve—Cold Cream—Eucalyptus
Salve—Flying Ointment or Seer Salve—Gombault's
Caustic Balsam—Holy Anointing Oil or Unguent—Honey
Balm—Insomnia Salve—Lip Balm 1—Lip Balm 2—Medea Salve—
Pomatum—Populeon—Sage and Violet Salve—St. John's Wort
Salve

MISCELLANY 119

Animal Hoof Oil—Pet Crumble—Wild Bird Feeder 1—Wild Bird
Feeder 2—Canine/Feline Ice Blocks—Canine/Feline Treats—
Travelers' Translations—Approximate Smoke Points of Oils

INTRODUCTION

*"Good cooking means the knowledge of all fruits,
herbs, balms, and spices, and all that is healing
and sweet in fields and groves, and savory in meats.
It means carefulness, inventiveness, watchfulness,
willingness, and readiness of appliances.
It means the economy of your great-grandmothers
and the science of modern chemists."*
—RUSKIN

The Culinary Library explores the history, tools, uses, and preparation techniques of the foods man has spent thousands of years domesticating. Once taken from the wild and cultivated, domesticated foods may vary in their popularity through the centuries, but they seldom revert to their wild state; in fact, just the opposite occurs because producers, scientists, and chefs invent better and greater varieties, textures, and flavors to capture our imaginations and add delight to our culinary world.

Alchemy of the Mortar and Pestle begins at the beginning by exploring the tool instrumental in man's domestication of food. The process of grinding and pounding plant material and flesh that we now call trituration predates man's use of fire for cooking, and, along with air drying, was probably our first food preparation technique.

It was made possible by the discovery of the first domestic tool, the mortar and pestle.

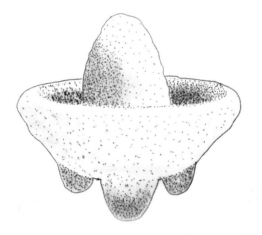

At its simplest level, a mortar and pestle is a tool for bashing and grinding; at its most sophisticated, it is a piece of modern art where form is everything and function redundant. Symbolically, it is both the masculine and the feminine, representing fertility, abundance, and the life force.

We define the mortar as a receptacle, usually but not always bowl shaped, in which food, ingredients, medicine, and matter (usually plant in origin) are placed ready for pounding and grinding. The word "mortar" derives from the Latin word *mortarium*, meaning "receptacle for pounding."

Its partner in destruction, the pestle, is a short rod or bat that is moved around either over or inside the Mortar in a downward and circular motion. The word "pestle" derives from the Latin word *pestillum*, meaning "pounder."

INTRODUCTION

Their purpose in coming together is to break down the molecular bonds of food and matter by grinding, pounding, and mixing. The process that occurs to particles caught between a mortar and pestle to break them apart and reduce their size is called trituration, a word coined in the mid-1600s, probably meaning "threshed." Modern French cooks have also invented a word to describe the process of trituration and use the verb *concasse* for the action.

Both mortar and pestle are traditionally made from nonbrittle, smooth materials that must be hard enough to withstand wear and tear, cohesive enough so no particles flake off to enter food, and nonporous so they do not absorb flavors or trap microorganisms. Materials include ceramic, glass, porcelain, stone (including granite, marble, basalt, or volcanic rock), wood, bamboo, iron, steel, brass, ivory, lead, and bronze.

Perhaps because it is prehistoric or because it is one of our oldest culinary tools, the mortar and pestle continues to vibrate a distant chord in our subconscious memory and capture our imaginations. This survival tool is one of man's earliest discoveries, probably earlier than fire or sharpened flint, where the simple act of bringing together two hard surfaces in friction began the refining and domestication of food that eventually transformed us from wild, nomadic hunter-gatherers to community-based grain harvesters, then to bread makers, and eventually to chefs.

At its lowest point in modern history, this iconic tool has been replaced by machines and pushed off the culinary shelf by our fast lifestyles and even faster foods. But despite changing fashions, this humble, unpretentious tool has managed to survive the industrial, machine, technological, information, and computer ages to remain in continuous use throughout thousands of years and across all major cultures of the world. The mortar and pestle is more popular today than at any other time in culinary history.

But cooks are consumers as well as producers, and deciding we must have a new tool in our kitchens is as inevitable as buying that next cookbook, just a matter of awareness and discovery. So we buy our new mortar and pestle and arrange it on the kitchen bench to be admired and discussed like some exotic artifact that only we have discovered. We pound a little garlic, some herbs, a few nuts, chilies and pesto, for a while at least. Then nothing. Despite our passion for creation and this interesting object, no inspiration rises up to overwhelm and overtake us. We watch TV chefs using them, their knowing smiles hinting at secret knowledge, their silent lips withholding their recipes.

There is no question we love owning our mortar and pestle, but...what...exactly...do we do with it now? The simple answer to this question, as with all others in life, is either everything or nothing. We can enjoy looking at it, or we can try our hand at magic, and either way we're right. For those who choose to experiment, there are some definite returns for the manual work involved.

As cooks we are eternally grateful for electric blenders, food processors, Thermomixers, and all the wonderful kitchen gadgets that take the tediousness out of cooking and make the art of the professional chef replicable by even the most amateur of cooks. But the disadvantage of using machines for all food processing is that they are not necessary for small amounts, and the higher friction and heat they generate mean that food aromas "burn off" and escape as gas. So for the mindful cook for whom the preparation of ingredients is a multisensory experience, only the ancient culinary tool of mortar and pestle can deliver the essential oil and flavor essences, where the crushing of fibrous plants, such as peels, ginger, lemongrass, and garlic, gives up greater depths as we exercise minute control over texture and intensity of flavor.

The process of transformation that occurs with the mortar and pestle is nothing less than alchemy.

Hermes Trismegistus, thought by some to be a myth and by others to be a living man some five thousand years BC in Egypt, is credited with the creation of a process we call alchemy. His cryptic recipe for the transformation of base matter to its most sublime or highest form is the stuff of legend and myth. Said to have been engraved onto green stone or a green gem, it was deemed so powerful and dangerous it was recorded in the form of a secret riddle, decipherable only by priests, kings, and pharaohs. This carved stone has become known as the Emerald Tablet, its carved message as the alchemical formula, and the end result as the Philosopher's Stone.

Hermes' seven steps to transmute a base matter into a heavenly one can be applied to mental health, turning base metals into gold, and many acts of creation and transformation. With the liberty of literary license, we can even apply the seven stages of alchemy to the mortar and pestle.

1. **Calcification**: The application of the initial friction creates heat and begins the breaking down of the cellular structure of the base material, usually plant matter.

2. **Dissolution** The continued application of force causes the water particles to begin separating and creates greater viscosity.

3. **Separation** The essential oil molecules break away from the solids and liquids, resulting in, and identified by, the release of aroma.

4. **Conjunction** Additional matter is introduced, broken down, and blended to create a union where the fragile beginnings of a new form take place.

5. **Fermentation** This is as much a process of the mind as of matter, where creative inspiration continues with the addition of and resting of ingredients. Focused imagination and gentle ingenuity begin to create new textures and tastes.

6. **Distillation** After the final ingredient is added, there is a last vigorous agitation before the blended amalgam or balsam becomes light and pure.

7. **Coagulation** The final product sits, rests, and its flavor sets.

Most ingredients used in these seven steps will be sour, sweet, pungent, or bitter, but for the final balance or perfection we need a fifth flavor. It comes to us from a further cryptic, often ignored, secret-eighth-step of alchemy, lost to many translations throughout history. This last hidden message says that once perfection is achieved, the master alchemist must work with the heavenly element of "salt." This was no doubt simply an order to the wise to preserve knowledge by passing their wisdom on to others, but we can see no valid reason why any culinary alchemist of the mortar and pestle should not take the word literally rather than symbolically. After all, salt is the only ingredient added to water, other than prayer and intention, to render it holy.

INTRODUCTION

So step eight, we say, is to add and balance your salt. Or, to paraphrase the words of Carl Jung, one of the world's great psychological alchemists, we do not know why we need salt, but we have to eat it to feel better.

For more information about the multiple choices and unique properties of various salts, see, The Culinary Library volume on salt and pepper.

Every food has its own distinctive flavor, texture, and strengths, and once you find the ones your palate prefers, you will find it difficult to use any other. Exploring the sources and varieties of ingredients and selecting them can involve thought, just as the choice to use a mortar and pestle requires a mindfulness no longer common in the modern world. We often avoid the responsibility of thinking about our food choices; we become lazy and relinquish this luxury to large companies because food is plentiful or because we use the excuse of affordability and availability. Because creating in the mortar and pestle requires only small quantities, we owe it to ourselves, and the planet, to take back our power and use the healthiest quality ingredients available.

May your journey through this book encourage you to take your mortar and pestle from whatever dim, dark culinary cupboard it has been assigned to and bring it back into the light, and, at the very least, offer you some ideas and additional uses for it. If you don't own one already, then this humble tool has surely earned its place in your kitchen. But be warned: the journey of the apprentice alchemist is not for the faint hearted, and only when you bring a sharp mind and a firm hand to this art will you create culinary potions to delight even the most jaded of palates.

For now, though, as with all true apprenticeships, we must go back and start at the very beginning.

HISTORY

———·•·◆·•·———

"History consists of a series of
accumulated imaginative inventions."
—VOLTAIRE

PREHISTORIC MAN ....
Cooks are imaginative creatures, so inventing a plausible prehistory year zero for our first culinary tool is easy.

We can safely assume that men created the prehistoric cave paintings. Why? Because no pictorial records have been found of culinary matters. There are wonderful depictions of the manly hunting side of life and the brave exploits of, bless their souls, our male ancestors who ventured out to spear protein. But, alas, there are no cave-painted records of the womanly side of prehistoric life, no visual record of the preparation and cooking of gathered foods, no depiction of the first stones used to crush flesh or the hard shells of crustacean and nut. The pride in the tools of the hunt is not accorded equally to the first domestic tool, which not only pounded meat and ground grain, but prepared the ochre paint that make those cave paintings possible.

So let's assume that one day long ago, in the dim dark time of Before, after returning from a successful hunt, the men of the tribe delivered their kill before retiring to the back of the communal cave to record their brave deeds.

The women, tired of sole parenting, keeping the fires going, defending the camp, and gathering food and water, were probably less than happy with the prospect of having to prepare a hot dinner. We can imagine them picking up heavy stones and then bashing down repeatedly on the stiff, cold, hairy carcass in sheer frustration, only to discover by total accident the tenderizing advantages of triturating their food.

Because a large flat stone is required to pound meat and grain, it lacks portability, but because of this the continuous friction of one stone over another over time creates a concave indentation, and this additional depth would have had the advantage of allowing the preparation of greater amounts and wetter foods and catching blood runoff. This was probably a big deal in the days when protein was on the hoof. The incentive to bring food to this tool would have increased the deeper and more useful it became, until the advantages of staying might have outweighed those of moving on, thereby encouraging settlement and the domestication of food. Others of the tribe, not just food gatherers and preparers but ochre grinders, medicine shamans, soothsayers, and dream weavers—the equivalents of today's chefs, artists, doctors, and priests—would soon have shared the use of this amazing invention.

Although archeology shows us that man's desire to change the form and texture of food and matter by pounding, mixing, and grinding has a continuous and unbroken history for many thousands of years, the earliest written records of the use of a recognizable mortar and pestle comes to us from as recently as three to four thousand years ago. The three surviving written records from this time are the Indian Book of Veda, from which Ayurvedic medicine is thought to originate, the Chinese Yellow Emperor's Book of Internal Medicine, and the Egyptian Ebers Papyrus.

THE INDIAN BOOK OF VEDA...........................

The Indian Veda is thought to be the oldest book known to humanity, written in Sanskrit and originating with the Aryans who occupied the Indus valley in the north of India before 2000 BC. The Aryans pushed the indigenous Dravidians south and then created the Indian caste system with the merging of their cultures, and it was the higher castes in the north who created the Vedic civilization and from whom we inherit the four books that make up the Veda. Only one of these books, the forth, known as Atharva Veda, links us to the use of the mortar and pestle, where it was used for preparing spells and medicines to ward off demons and diseases of both the body and spirit. The forth book of Veda was black and white magic for everyday life, using plants like ginger, opium, and black branching fungi, and having incantations to cure everything from toothaches to curses. The Veda charm against intestinal worms, for example, says:

"With Indra's great mill stone, that crushes all vermin, do I grind to pieces these worms" and "as lentils with a mill stone...we grind to pieces with our charm."

Also, in India's history, we find other references to the common use of the mortar and pestle; short-grain rice being pounded to separate the rice grain from its husk and to make flour for the pancake known as chapattis; ancient zinc-lead mines in the northwestern state of Rajasthan using giant mortars carved into the hard exposed rock face of the mines, and two-man pestles to crush zinc ore and quartz rock to extract gold. From the fourth century BC, several ancient Jain Sutras were compiled with masi made by grinding burnt bone, tar, pitch, and hide glue. Masi was later renamed by the Colonial English as Indian ink.

THE YELLOW EMPEROR'S BOOK OF INTERNAL MEDICINE ....

From ancient China a document survives known as "The Yellow Emperor's Book of Internal Medicine," thought to date from around 2000 BC but possibly relating to and based on an earlier document called the Neijing, written some six hundred to seven hundred years earlier. The Yellow Emperor's Book has two major texts, each comprising eighty-one chapters, all written as a mythical conversation between a fictional character called the Yellow Emperor and his six equally fictitious ministers.

Book One explains the Chinese practice of basic medicine, and Book Two, the practice and philosophy of acupuncture. Combined, they are the major texts of the Daoist theory now called the Tao. Unlike the Book of Veda, the Yellow Emperor texts attribute illness not to demonic spirit influence, but to the effects of diet, lifestyle, emotion, environment, and age. It introduces us to the concepts of the forces of yin and yang; chi and qi energy; the five elements of the body, of hot, cold, warm, cool, and neutral; and the five tastes of the palate, sour, bitter, pungent, sweet, and salty. A man's life was seen as a mirror of the balance or imbalance of these things, and book one gives recipes for grinding and mixing healing tinctures and magical potions using ingredients like myrrh, sandalwood, coriander, and ginger. The Yellow Emperor also makes the claim that he is the original inventor of the mortar and pestle.

THE EGYPTIAN EBERS PAPYRUS ....

Some 450 years later, around 1550 BC, we find the mortar and pestle reference trail leads us to ancient Egypt, where a papyrus was written mentioning "the unguent makers." They were described as the preparers of the magical scents (elixirs) and secret mixtures (potions) used by the priests and pharaohs in their religious and temple rituals. At that time in history, there was no distinction between the words that described the role of priest, magician, and healer. The papyrus survived and was purchased in 1862 by an American antiquarian-adventurer living in Egypt at the time named Edwin Smith. Its provenance reported it was found between the legs of a mummy in the Assassif area of the Necropolis on the west bank of the Nile opposite the old capital of Thebes. Eleven years later, in 1873, for some unknown reason, Smith sold it to a German Egyptologist, Georg Ebers, and thereafter it became known as the Ebers Papyrus.

As well as the mention of ancient Egyptian unguent makers, there is the reference to their tool, the mortar and pestle, and some of their seven hundred recipes with common ingredients, including myrrh, frankincense, cardamom, dill, fennel, and thyme. From these master alchemists of the mortar and pestle came magical pastes, salves, elixirs, and potions which were used not only to treat a myriad of ills, such as arthritis, depression, skin diseases, intestinal worms, chronic headache, toenail pain, and crocodile bite, but also to attract lovers or enhance communion with the gods.

The Ebers Papyrus is arguably the world's most important early record of plant usage in medicine. Measuring over twenty meters long and the equivalent of 110 pages of text, it details in hieroglyphs the ancient medical recipes to cure both physical and spiritual ills. The papyrus text refers specifically to the ninth year of the reign of Pharaoh Amenhotep I, which dates it to around 1534 BC, although there is some thought that it is a copy of an even earlier medical work attributed to a priest called Thoth, writing around 3000 BC and in active use in 2800 BC in the reign of Khufu. Khufu's pyramid is the largest of the three pyramids built next to the Sphinx on the plane of Giza, Cairo. The Ebers Papyrus is now held in the University of Leipzig library.

MEXICAN AZTECS ....

In Mexico, the mortar and pestle are well known from the archeology of an ancient civilization that lived six thousand years ago in the Tehuacan Valley. The name now used to describe it is *molcajete y tejolote*, thought possibly to derive from the Aztec language, Nahuatl, where *molcajete* (or mortar) derives from the words *moili* (liquid/sauce) and *caxitl* (bowl) and *tejolote* (or pestle) from the words *tetl* (stone) and *xototi* (doll), meaning a bowl for making liquid or sauce using a stone doll. Perhaps there is also a male/female connection here as well. There is some evidence that the earliest sacrificial temples and giant pounders were used to decapitate and catch the blood of captured prisoners.

Traditionally the large Mexican mortar and pestle is made of a black lava stone called basalt, where the surface is rough and textured but the stone very hard and nonporous. It is used for making pesto, whose name dervives from "pestle" or "pounding," and for making guacamole, ground chilies, and for grinding roasted cacao nibs for chocolate.

THE OLD TESTAMENT AND BIBLICAL TIMES ....

Written seventeen hundred years after the Ebers Papyrus, the Old Testament mentions the mortar and pestle being in use in ancient Jerusalem. In the fourth book of Moses, called Numbers, in chapter 11, verses 7 and 8, we read, "And the manna was as coriander seed, and the color thereof as the color of bdellium. And the people went about, and gathered it, and ground it in mills, or beat it in a mortar, and baked it in pans, and made cakes of it, and the taste of it was the taste of fresh oil." Also in the Old Testament, in Proverbs chapter 27, verse 22, we are advised, "Though thou shouldest bray (beat) a fool in a mortar among wheat with a pestle, yet will not his foolishness depart from him." There is mention also of the users being called the "compounders of unguents," and in the days of Nehemiah we learn there was a whole street of unguent makers in ancient Jerusalem. In the modern version of the Bible, this is often referred to as the Street of the Apothecaries, an early name for the trade of today's chemists, whose guild symbol remains the mortar and pestle. One of the roles of these unguent makers, we are told, was to pound and grind roots and herbs with oils and incense to produce "holy oils," and in the days of Christ this trade was hereditary and was passed from father to son, as in the Abtinas family.

Some of the elixirs and balms mentioned from biblical times have been passed down through the generations and are still known, like the balm of Gilead, the ointment of King Agrippa of Judea, and the seer balm or flying ointment which is still made today and sought after by meditators and spiritual seekers wishing to communicate with the Divine. Ancient recipes, with a little source sleuthing, are still within the reach of any mortar and pestle enthusiast. Details of these can be found in later chapters.

ANCIENT ROME ....
The Romans were familiar with the mortar and pestle, and the poet Jurenal describes the preparation of "drugs" or "medicines" with a *mortarium* and *pistillum*. And the ancient Roman cookbook known as 'Apicius' has recipes including one for grinding caraway, cumin, pepper, bay, dates, honey, vinegar, and oil for anointing the roasting dormice.

AMERICAN INDIANS ....
Bowl-like indentations have been found ground in flat rock surfaces in early American Indian settlements, where it is believed they were used to grind acorns, nuts, and corn. The smaller, mobile stone mortar was called a *metate* and the pestle a *mano*, and some of these original tools are still available for sale today, with archeological provenance, selling for a couple of hundred dollars up to thousands, depending on their size and condition.

EUROPEAN AND ENGLISH APOTHECARIES ......
Italian frescoes exist from the fifteenth century depicting the mortar and pestle being used in apothecaries. Europeans have used materials as divergent as brass, copper, ceramic, marble, and wood.

In 1779, the Wedgwood mortar and pestle was made with the base of the pestle and the mortar made from the finest porcelain, with the handle of the pestle made of wood. These became and remained the most popular set with apothecaries and chemists worldwide until specialist groups of chemists formed and began the bulk manufacture of medications, salves, and unguents, beginning a new industry that later became known as pharmaceutical companies.

ASIA ....

The Japanese developed a distinctive mortar called a *suribachi*, made of glazed, ridged earthenware, and a pestle called a *surikogi*, made from wood. Its uses include grinding sesame seeds and reducing meat and seafood to pastes.

Indian mortars and pestles have generally been made of brass and used for spice mixing, and in Hindu ceremonies for weddings and upanayanam when turmeric is crushed. However, in the more remote northwestern mountain regions, they are used to thrash grain, and the mortar is large enough to hold three individual pestles working in unison and rhythm.

In Malaysia the mortar and pestle is called a *kesung*, and in Southeast Asia it is usually made of granite and used in the grinding of pungent spices and chili pastes.

The Indonesian *cobek* and *ulek ulek* are made of basalt or palm wood with a dish-shaped mortar and an unusually shaped, right-angled pestle.

RUSSIA ....

In Russian and Slavic folklore, there is a witchlike hag called Baba Yaga, who flies out of her chimney to kidnap little children. Her transport is a mortar, and she stands in it using the pestle as either a rudder or a paddle.

THE MIDDLE EAST ....

In the Middle East, mortars can be very large, bucket-sized affairs, made of stone and with wooden pestles some two to three feet long, traditionally used to grind meat for kibbeh or chickpeas and sesame seeds for hummus.

SELECTION

"The artist is the only one who knows that the world is a subjective creation, that there is a choice to be made, a selection of elements"
—ANAIS NIN

Selecting your mortar and pestle is simple and purely a matter of personal preference and availability. With the Internet to help you shop worldwide, you can now buy anything you prefer that you can afford. Buying your mortar and pestle is simpler than buying other culinary tools, especially electrical appliances, because all mortars and pestles you own will have the same maximum power, speed, and endurance—i.e., you.

Once you have decided you *must* have one, there's no turning back, and the only decision you will have to make is whether to buy it for yourself or ask for one as a present. My advice is to buy your own, because the material your set is made from and the size you require are individual to you.

If you just want to grind tablets and medication to make them quicker to assimilate or easier to swallow, then you may want to consider a small glass or porcelain set.

If you want to use your mortar and pestle as a kitchen tool, then go for a bigger one.

In general the rule is, the larger the set, the more it holds, the heavier it weighs.

So if you are in frail health or prone to dropping things, avoid the big granite or stone ones and go for wood. Better to break the mortar than your foot. Having said that, the larger sets are usually more stable to use, and the greater depth is useful if you are impatient, like me, or want to grind larger quantities or have the versatility of wetter mixtures. If you opt for a lighter one, it's a good idea to stand it on a nonslip mat, a tea towel, or washcloth to stop it moving about if you get enthusiastic and carried away in the moment.

It is possible to find beautiful mortars and pestles in designer kitchen and produce stores in all capital cities of the world, and they can cost anywhere up to $1,000.

In our view, there are better uses for your money, because in most cases sets made from identical materials and of the same size can be purchased at your local Asian grocery or chain-store kitchen shop for a small fraction of the cost. If you spend over $50, you are really only paying for a product that either carries a designer label or has an unusual shape, like the flat mortars and inverted mushroom pestles we've seen about recently. They are very beautiful and exquisitely designed, but in our opinion they are more art than function. There can be nothing sadder to us than a mortar and pestle that can never truly fulfill its core purpose in life. The mortar and pestle we currently use is eight inches (twenty centimeters) wide and five inches (thirteen centimeters) deep, is made of smooth black granite, is heavier than the average cat at seven kilograms, and cost us $40 in the Asian markets.

And then, we guess, there are those of you who just can't help yourselves, have an irresistible urge to spend lots of money, and don't want to miss out. If this sounds like you, why not consider buying more than one? Have several different sizes and shapes from different cultures. If you prefer really old ones, you can spend your days searching the Web or antique stores for historical sets that will be rich with the patina of age and long lives of magical service. It always surprises us how little the really old authentic sets sell for compared to some of the new designer sets. For that same $1,000 at the trendy store, you can buy yourself several amazing sets from the eighteenth and nineteenth centuries. That's the 1700s and 1800s! And there are even earlier ones, many hundreds or thousands of years old, with provenance, from archeological digs.

If you like to travel, no matter where you go in the world, be it Mexico or Paris, Cairo or Sydney, Delhi or Bali, sleuthing the local markets, exotic bazaars, antique and ultramodern shops will take on a whole new excitement and meaning. Remember, you'll need to know the names of the mortar and pestle in the local languages so the sellers will know what you are searching for. Asking for a mortar and pestle in Penang or Malacca will get you only blank stares, whereas asking for a kesung may get you a beaming smile and into the back room, behind the dusty boxes, to where the real treasure has been hiding for a hundred years or more. We've included a translated list in the "Miscellany" section at the end of the book; just photocopy and take with you on your next exotic travel adventure.

If you have already bought or have been given a new mortar and pestle set, there are a couple of things you will need to do before you get down to the serious business of the alchemy of culinary potions. Just like any new utensil, the mortar and pestle should be cleaned and seasoned before use.

1. Wash in clean water without detergent and air-dry.
2. Grind roughly a small handful of white rice. Discard and repeat if necessary until the rice remains white and does not discolor. This will depend on the type of material your set is made from.
3. Add 4 cloves of garlic, 1 teaspoon cumin, 1 teaspoon salt, and 1 teaspoon pepper. Grind and discard.
4. Wash in clean water without detergent and air-dry.

NB: If you already have a set and missed these steps, don't panic. It just means that whoever ate your first efforts probably ingested some stone dust, minigravel, or wood shavings. It will be long gone by now with the subject none the wiser, and it will not affect the ongoing performance of your set. Only you, your enthusiasm, and your passion can do that.

Once you are ready to start, a good rule to remember is:
- Driest ingredients first.
- Moist ones next.
- Oily ones next.
- Wet ones next.
- Taste and add salt to your work if needed.

Never use detergent or soap to clean your set, as perfume particles can be minute and may be absorbed and taint your food.

To sanitize stone, heat occasionally in the oven at 350°F/180°C for ten minutes. Make sure to leave the mortar and pestle to cool in the oven, door open, once it's turned off. Never try and lift out a heavy, hot stone or you may do more damage than break a toe.

When you're ready, decide what you're going to make first. It doesn't matter if it's something simple like crushing strawberries, or a few nuts and oil to make peanut butter for your morning toast, or a complex sauce with twenty ingredients. You might make a mess or you might not. You might try too hard and end up with a too-fine paste or a sore wrist. You might even add some new smears to your cupboards or swear words to your vocabulary. Whatever happens, relax and remember, even the master chefs have had to begin at the beginning, and all good apprentices see their mistakes as opportunities to learn..

You are now a student in Alchemy 101, and if you become a master or not does not matter a fig. (I'm sure the Veda masters' complex mortar and pestle recipe for regaining a lost emperorship didn't work every time.) The important thing, symbolically anyway, is that you have embraced an infinitesimally small part of a mysterious, magical practice that began in the Before, in the prehistory of time, and one that will continue to eternity as long as there are two particles left in the universe to rub together.

RECPES

"Tell me what you eat, I'll tell you who you are."
—ANTHELME BRILLAT-SAVARIN

For all recipes, garlic count is peeled and in cloves, anchovy count is in preserved fillets, and flaked salt is not rock salt. Chili means fresh, deseeded, long and spicy, not short and dangerous, and sugar generally is for any natural sweetener, e.g., honey, natural cane sugar, molasses, agave nectar, date sugar, brown rice syrup, maple syrup, pomegranate molasses, but not artificial substitutes. Bread crumbs means fresh or dried, herbs means leaves and stalks except for coriander, which includes roots as well, and mint, which is leaves only. Nuts are roasted and shelled, pepper is cracked or whole, white, black, pink, or green. Cheese is grated, fruit is stoneless, spices are lightly toasted or roasted. The method of mixing is for you to decide, but try grinding dry ingredients first, then add moist, then wet ingredients.

SAUCES

AIOLI ....

4 garlic cloves
Flaked salt
1 teaspoon Dijon mustard
(An option is to add 2 tablespoons quince paste at this stage.)
1 egg yolk
Slowly drizzle in ½ cup olive oil while mixing.
1 teaspoon lemon juice
½ teaspoon cold water
Slowly drizzle in an additional ½ cup olive oil.
Should be the consistency of mayonnaise.
Great with pasta, meat, crudités, vegetable, salads, chicken, fish.

ALMOND SAUCE ....

1 cup almonds
1 teaspoon cinnamon
2-3 mint leaves
1 anchovy
1 teaspoon lemon juice
½ cup bread crumbs
½ to ¾ cup olive oil
Serve with chicken or fish.

ANCHOVY SAUCE ....
1 garlic clove
1 fresh, deseeded, chili pepper or less if you prefer
¼ cup parsley
1 teaspoon sugar
1 teaspoon capers
1 teaspoon tomato puree
Anchovy to taste

AUBERGINE SAUCE ....
1 teaspoon chili powder or 2 teaspoons chili sauce or 1 fresh, finely chopped, long red chili
½ teaspoon celery salt
2 finely chopped shallots or 1 finely chopped red onion
3 garlic cloves
1 tablespoon black onion seeds
1 teaspoon ground fenugreek seeds
8-10 fresh mint leaves
2 tablespoon tomato paste
100 milliliters cream, crème fraiche, or sour cream
Salt/pepper
Mix all the above ingredients together in the mortar and pestle and then add to 400 grams hot aubergine cubes or thin slices sautéed first in oil until soft and caramelized. Heat together for a few additional minutes until the spice mix has cooked. Then add 150 milliliters of chicken or vegetable stock. Simmer until it is the consistency you prefer and serve hot or cold with chicken, game, legumes (such as peas, beans, or lentils), or pasta.

BERRY SAUCE ....

Any soft seasonal berries can be crushed in the mortar. The amount depends on the size of your mortar but most will hold at least 1 punnet (pint). A few drops of balsamic vinegar or kirsch will enhance the flavor of the berries even more, and they can sit happily crushed and liquefied and steeping in your mortar for hours. Assuming you can keep everyone from tasting them, simply spoon them at the last minute over, under, or around desserts, into cocktails, or as a plate garnish around meat, chicken, or crustacean dishes. And if there are any left over, you might have to make pancakes or crispy cream waffles for breakfast.

BREAD SAUCE ....

4 garlic cloves
1 finely chopped onion
2 bay leaves
1 tablespoon green peppercorns, brine drained
Grated Nutmeg
Salt
150 grams fresh white bread crumbs
4 tablespoons fresh cream
25 grams butter

Mix all together in the mortar and pestle and then stir and heat in a small saucepan with 2-3 tablespoons melted butter. When the garlic, onion, and crumbs begin to caramelize, toast, and take on color, blend in 450 milliliters of cream. Bring slowly to a gentle rolling boil, stirring to incorporate as it heats. Check the seasoning before serving.

This amazing, often neglected sauce is wonderful with all roasts and all manner of grilled and barbecued meats and fish. It can also be easily turned into a tasty soup by extension. Just add milk, chicken stock powder or cubes, and some additional cubes of white bread. Serve hot with a drizzle of cream, chopped parsley or chives, and toasted croutons and/or grated cheese.

BUTTERSCOTCH SAUCE ....

75 grams butter
150 grams brown sugar
175 grams canned evaporated milk or cream
Mix all together into a smooth liquid in the mortar and pestle.
Then stir until it comes to a boil in a small saucepan. Stop when it thickens and colors to the consistency you like.
Serve hot and sweet over pancakes, waffles, muffins, cakes, fruit pies, stewed fruit, tarts, ice cream, or yogurt. You can also use this in pastry cups and top with marshmallow or meringue.

COCONUT CORIANDER SAUCE ....

25 grams fresh gingerroot
Zest of 1 lemon or lime
1 cup coriander leaves and stems
2 bay leaves
15 grams butter
2 tablespoons plain (all-purpose) flour
2 teaspoons castor (superfine) sugar
Salt/pepper
Grind together in the mortar and pestle, then heat gently in a small saucepan before stirring in 400 milliliters coconut milk. When simmered, serve with grilled chicken or fish.

CREAMY SORREL SAUCE ....

1 cup sorrel

2 finely chopped shallots or baby onions

2 tablespoons plain (all-purpose) flour

Salt/pepper

Grated nutmeg

40 grams butter

When mixed together to a paste, add to 150 milliliters of cream heated with 150 milliliters of white wine. Stir until it comes gently to the boil. Serve with fish, chicken or lamb.

GARLIC SAUCE ....

10 garlic cloves soaked in boiling water for 10 minutes, drained

2 anchovies

Small handful capers

Flaked salt

5 peppercorns

3 tablespoons white wine vinegar

½-⅔ cup olive oil

Serve over hard-boiled eggs or salads.

GARLIC-ROSEMARY SAUCE ....

12 garlic cloves
3 tablespoons chopped rosemary
1 teaspoon sugar
1 teaspoon flaked salt
A few mint leaves
½ teaspoon black peppercorns
A splash of lemon juice or vinegar
Serve with lamb.

GARLIC-WALNUT SAUCE ....

2 garlic cloves
1 cup walnut meat
1-2 slices white bread soaked with 2 tablespoons red wine vinegar,
2 tablespoons lemon juice, and 2 tablespoons water
4 tablespoons olive oil
Allspice, pepper, salt
Serve mixed into any hot green vegetables, over potatoes, arti-
chokes, and tomatoes, or with roast chicken.

GREEN SAUCE NO. 1 ....

2 garlic cloves
1 fresh, green, deseeded chili or less if you prefer
1-2 cups parsley
1-2 anchovies
½ cup bread crumbs
1 tablespoon red wine vinegar
⅔ cup olive oil

GREEN SAUCE NO. 2 ....

3 tablespoons pine nuts
3 green olives, pitted
1 garlic clove
Salt
1 tablespoon capers
1 anchovy
1 hard-boiled egg yolk
½ cup bread crumbs
1 cup parsley
1 tablespoon lemon juice or vinegar
½ cup olive oil
Serve with boiled meat.

HONEY-SOY SAUCE ....

2 tablespoons honey plus 2 tablespoons sugar
2 tablespoons soy sauce plus 2 tablespoons fish sauce
4 tablespoons mirin or rice wine vinegar

HORSERADISH SAUCE ....

1 cup fresh, washed, peeled, grated horseradish root
½ cup white bread crumbs
2 tablespoons white wine vinegar
Salt
Store in a jar in the fridge with a little olive oil on top. Serve as is
or mixed with a little fresh cream.

LEMON SAUCE ....

2 garlic cloves
2 tablespoons oregano
4 tablespoons parsley
Salt/pepper
Juice of 1-2 lemons
½ cup olive oil
Can add Dijon mustard as an optional extra.
Serve over fish.

PAD THAI SAUCE ....

¼ cup dry roasted peanuts, salted or unsalted, skins off
1 garlic clove
1 cup coriander, fresh
1 tablespoon brown sugar
1 tablespoon chili sauce or 1 teaspoon fresh chili
2 tablespoons (heaped) chopped spring onions
2 tablespoons mirin or rice wine vinegar
2 tablespoons peanut or olive oil
2 tablespoons fish sauce
2 tablespoons lime juice
When mixed, heat in a fry pan and add 200 grams of rice stick noodles that have been soaked for 5 minutes in boiling water and drained. Top with bean sprouts, coriander, fried tofu puffs, fried spring onion, and cracked peanuts. (For kids, call this Nuts on Noodle Mountain.)

PARSLEY SAUCE ....

1 cup fresh parsley
25 grams plain (all-purpose) flour
25 grams butter
Salt/pepper
Ground Nutmeg
When mixed, heat gently for a few minutes and then add 250 milliliters of chicken or fish or beef stock, 250 milliliters milk, and 3 tablespoons cream. Stir to avoid lumps while it comes to the boil. Serve with boiled ham, silverside or corned beef, fish, chicken, boiled potatoes, or steamed vegetables.

PEANUT SAUCE ....

1 cup dry roasted peanuts, unsalted, skins off
2 garlic cloves
2 tablespoons brown sugar
½ cayenne pepper (or 1 teaspoon chili sauce)
½ teaspoon tamarind paste (or ½ tablespoon lime juice)
2 tablespoons fish sauce
1 teaspoon soy sauce
2 teaspoons sesame oil
⅓ cup coconut cream
⅓ cup water
Use for chicken, lamb, or beef satay, dipping or drizzling.

PESTO SAUCE ....

1-2 garlic cloves
1-2 cups basil leaves
1 cup pine nuts or walnuts or almonds
Flaked salt
¼ cup grated Parmigiano-Reggiano cheese
¼ cup Pecorino-Romano cheese
¼-½ cup olive oil, drizzled in last
Serve with pasta, crudités, or on bruschetta.

PISTACHIO SAUCE ....

1 garlic clove
1 lemon, zest and juice
1 cup shelled, unsalted pistachio nuts
½ cup chopped parsley
A few mint leaves
1 tablespoon orange blossom water
Black peppercorns and salt flakes
6 tablespoons olive oil
½ teaspoon sugar
Water to taste
Serve with lamb, chicken, fish, falafel, as a dip for pita, on bruschetta with ham, pears, feta, etc.

PLUM SAUCE ··

½ teaspoon five spice powder
2 tablespoons brown sugar
1 small shallot, finely chopped
Zest of 1 lemon or lime
8 canned damson plums, drained and stones removed
Salt/pepper
4 tablespoons plum juice reserved from the can
Heat in a small pan before checking the seasoning and serving with cooked pork, lamb, duck, venison, or adding to gravies or casseroles.

POMEGRANATE SAUCE ·······························

Seeds of 1 pomegranate or 2 tablespoons pomegranate molasses
1 teaspoon brown sugar or ½ teaspoon castor sugar
1 tablespoon maple syrup
¼ teaspoon ground cinnamon
4 tablespoons olive oil
1 tablespoon water
Salt/black pepper
Drizzle on salads, fish, chicken, barbecued quail, spinach.

PRAWN/SHRIMP COCKTAIL SAUCE ··············

Equal quantities of cream and tomato sauce/ ketchup mixed together, seasoned with pepper and salt, then flavored with Worcestershire sauce, tabasco and lemon juice to suit your taste.

ROUX (see also Beurre Manie in Compound Butters) ····

Roux is a blend of equal amounts of butter and flour that is cooked before liquid is added. Its starting base is the compound butter beurre manie. Cooking eliminates the floury taste and allows the gluten in the flour to expand and therefore thicken other liquids. Making roux blanc or white sauces calls for cooking the beurre manie to the smell of fresh cream but not coloring it. Making roux blonde or pale honey-colored sauces calls for cooking beurre manie to the color of pale gold; this imparts a buttery flavor to soups and stews and gives them a sheen as well as thickening them. Beurre manie cooked to a light, hazelnutty-smelling brown, usually in the oven, is called roux brun or brown sauce, and this is used to thicken rich brown sauces such as demi-glace or espagnole. Adding warm milk infused with tarragon, chervil, shallot, thyme, and bay, then nutmeg, salt, and pepper to roux blanc and heating further creates a basic Béchamel sauce; adding cheese to this Béchamel creates a Mornay sauce, and adding cooked onion to Béchamel sauce creates the delicious Soubise sauce, etc.

SAFFRON CREAM SAUCE ....
½ teaspoon saffron threads into the mortar with 2 tablespoons boiling water or stock
Sit and infuse for 5-10 minutes
1 tablespoon plain (all-purpose) flour
15 grams butter
Salt/pepper
2 teaspoons lemon juice
75 milliliters cream
Heat the mix gently in a saucepan for a few minutes and then stir in 300 milliliter of chicken or fish stock, whisking or stirring until it comes to a boil.
Spoon over cooked fish, shellfish, chicken, or mix into cooked pasta. Finish with fresh chopped herbs.

SWEET AND SOUR SAUCE ....

½ cup sugar

½ cup vinegar

Fish sauce to taste

Fresh coriander

Soy sauce to taste

Pound, then reduce over heat. Thicken with ½ teaspoon arrow-root or corn flour if desired.

TAHINI SAUCE ....

2 garlic cloves

3 tablespoons tahini paste (the pale, water-hulled type, preferably)

Juice of ½ lemon

Salt, pepper, and water to taste

Use over all vegetables, salads, fish, skewered meats, barbecue, pulses (legumes), and beans.

TARRAGON SAUCE ....

3 garlic cloves

2 cups tarragon

A few basil leaves

Salt/pepper

2 pieces crustless bread soaked in white wine

or white wine vinegar

½ cup olive oil

Serve with chicken.

TARTARE SAUCE ....

¾ cup mayonnaise

½ teaspoon yellow mustard

½ teaspoon honey
½ teaspoon lemon zest + 4 of juice
Salt/pepper
½ finely chopped onion or capers
1 finely chopped pickle

WALNUT SAUCE ....

2 cups walnuts
½ cup pine nuts
½ small garlic clove
2-3 sage or marjoram leaves
¼ cup grated Parmigiano-Reggiano cheese
1 slice soft white bread, soaked in milk
½ cup olive oil
Serve with pasta, chicken, fish, and hot or cold meat.

WALNUT VINAIGRETTE ....

2 garlic cloves
2 tablespoons tarragon
5-6 tablespoons walnuts
¼ teaspoon flaked salt
¼ teaspoon black peppercorns
4 teaspoons sugar
2 teaspoons Worcestershire sauce
1 tablespoon Dijon mustard
1 tablespoon lemon juice
5 tablespoons vinegar (raspberry or pomegranate flavor is good)
½ cup walnut oil or 1 cup olive oil
Use on all types of salads and with crusty bread.

CURRIES, SPICES, AND PASTES

"There are many miracles in the world to be celebrated and, for me, garlic is the most deserving."
—LEO BUSCAGLIA

ALMOND PASTE ....
Grind 1 cup almonds to meal and add ½ cup powdered or icing sugar. In a small saucepan, heat 1 cup water with ¼ cup castor or granulated sugar and ¼ cup corn syrup. Stir only while bringing to the boil, then allow to boil for 3-5 minutes without stirring until a soft ball forms when a little of the mixture is dropped from a spoon into cold water. Do not allow to color. Cool and add to the almonds in the mortar. Mix together. If you want a richer paste, you can add beaten egg and/or heavy cream a tablespoon at a time, mixing until you have the consistency you require. Ratio of ground almonds to sugar is 1:1 for almond paste. Used in many pastry desserts. Great in a sweet pastry case, with or without fruit topping, and finished with Italian meringue. As Italian meringue uses the same soft-ball sugar syrup, just double the amount above and then drizzle and beat half the syrup into 4 egg whites that have already been brought to glossy peaks with ½ teaspoon cream of tartar. Once all the syrup is incorporated, you'll need to beat until the mixture cools and use without cooking further, or brown under the grill or with a gas gun (small propane torch).

CHILI PASTE ....

4 garlic cloves

4 chilies

4 tablespoons vinegar

Salt/pepper

DATE AND ORANGE BLOSSOM PASTE ....

Bruise 10-15 pitted dates in the mortar.

Cover with hot milk and leave to soak until cool.

Grind to a paste, then add:

1 tablespoon almonds, crushed or meal

1 teaspoon cinnamon

1-2 tablespoons orange blossom water (or any flower water, e.g., rosewater)

Serve as a dipping sauce for sweet biscuits or a filling for pastries or tarts.

DUKKAH SPICE ....

This Egyptian blend of seeds, nuts, and spice has a gentle flavor which pairs well with crusty bread. Dip it in strong olive oil and then the dukkah. There are many variations, but the following is representative of the more common style.

3 tablespoons sesame seeds

2 tablespoons hazelnuts

2 tablespoons almonds

1 tablespoon coriander seeds

1 tablespoon cumin seeds

(Dry-roasting nuts and seeds before use helps release the flavors.)

Grind the nuts and seeds together in the mortar and pestle and then add:

1 tablespoon pink salt flakes
1 tablespoon cracked black pepper
Try coating fresh fish with dukkah before frying.

EGG YOLK PASTE ....

This is a very old cook's trick from the Middle Ages. Make a basic paste by grinding together 150 milliliters thick cream with 2 raw egg yolks. Once thoroughly mixed together with the mortar and pestle, it can then be added gradually to soups or stews just before final serving but long enough to heat through. This adds a luscious, thickening richness. Coconut cream can be substituted for the dairy cream for Asian dishes. Make sure the yolks are well blended to avoid any lumps in the final dish.

GUACAMOLE ....

From Mexico, this creamy paste is used as a dip, a topping for toast and bruschetta, or on chili beans or tacos.
¼ small diced red onion
½ diced red tomato
Flesh from 2 ripe avocados
½ cup coriander, fresh
Salt/pepper
½ lemon, juice only

HARISSA ....

From the Middle East, harissa is a red, pungent spice mix with the bite of chili. It is used with grilled meat, fish, or chicken, mixed with rice or tabbouleh, added to soups, or used as a dip.
Toast 1 teaspoon coriander seed, 1 teaspoon cumin seed, and 1 teaspoon caraway.

Grind with:
3 garlic cloves
Pepper
2 red chilies
2 chopped red peppers
Fresh coriander and fresh mint
Salt

HERB SALTS ....
Sea or flaked salt
Dried herbs if you wish to store; fresh or dried and fresh combined
if using same or next day
Use a single herb or any combination, e.g., thyme, marjoram, kale,
parsley, celery, oregano, garlic, basil, fennel, leek, mountain pepper, lemon myrtle, aniseed myrtle, shallot tops, tarragon, cumin,
coriander, caraway.
Either add to dishes or serve in a small bowl on the table.

HUMMUS ....
This famous, fabulous, Moorish Lebanese dipping paste is heaven
on toast, with meat, vegetable dishes, bruschetta, sandwiches, or
salads, or just eaten from the spoon.
2 garlic cloves
½ small chopped onion
1 drained and very well-washed can of chickpeas, removing all the
preserved liquid (or 1 cup of dried chickpeas, soaked overnight,
well cooked, softened, and drained)
2-4 tablespoons olive oil
2 tablespoons lemon juice
1 tablespoon parsley
Grind all ingredients to a smooth paste, then taste and salt carefully.
Then, to soften and lighten, add cold water slowly, 1 tablespoon at

a time, mixing until the paste is smooth and creamy but not runny. This last step is often neglected by commercial producers and is the secret to a luscious and creamy hummus. Not only does it make the hummus lighter in color and melt-in-the-mouth soft, but it lifts the pungent garlic/sour lemon flavor to the front of the palate and away from the blandness of the chickpeas. For variety, fresh or frozen soy beans or broad beans (fava) can be used instead of chickpeas, but they must be well cooked and peeled before use.

MARZIPAN ....

4 tablespoons ground almonds
1 tablespoon icing (powdered) sugar
1 tablespoon castor sugar
1 raw egg yolk
A drop of vanilla essence (extract) and almond essence (extract)
Ratio of almonds to sugar is 2:1.

MASSAMAN CURRY PASTE ....

2 red seeded chilies (5 inches long), roughly chopped
1 piece lemongrass, chopped, white stalk only
1-inch piece galangal, chopped
4 coriander sets, stems & roots included (½ cup)
5 cloves
5 garlic cloves
5 cardamom seeds, paper shucks removed
4 shallots
1 teaspoon cinnamon
1 teaspoon shrimp paste
Salt

MOROCCAN NUT PASTE (AMLOU) ....

A delicious Moroccan nut spread or dip similar to peanut paste
(butter), but much more exotic and addictive.

½ cup roast almonds, salted

¼ cup hazelnuts

2 tablespoons honey

3-4 tablespoons argan oil (or substitute 3 tablespoons of olive oil
and one of dark sesame oil)

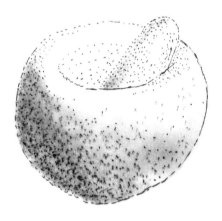

OLIVE PASTE (TAPENADE) ....

1 cup pitted black or green olives

3 tablespoons virgin olive oil

Pinch flaked salt

OLIVE AND CAPER PASTE ....

2 garlic cloves
2 tablespoons capers
2 tablespoons black olives
2 tablespoons green olives
2 tablespoons cognac
2 tablespoons oil
2 tablespoons lemon juice

OLIVE AND DATE PASTE ....

2 garlic cloves
½ cup chopped dates
½ cup black olives
¼ cup walnuts
¼ red chili
1 tablespoon chopped rosemary
1 tablespoon oil

PICADA ....

This is a Spanish paste used for thickening and adding color and richness to sauces, stews, and one-pot dishes.
½ cup blanched almonds
4 or 5 hard-boiled egg yolks
4 or 5 saffron threads infused in 1 tablespoon warm water
If you do not have saffron, ½ teaspoon sweet Spanish paprika can be substituted.
Add at the last minute, just before serving, to braised chicken, soups, stews, fish dishes, etc.

PISTOU ....

4 garlic cloves
1 cup fresh basil
2 tablespoons tomato paste or 6 tablespoons fresh tomato puree
3 tablespoons parmesan cheese
3-5 tablespoons olive oil
Flaked salt
Mix to a paste and add to pistou soup just before serving. Pistou is a French provincial broth soup made with carrots, potatoes, green beans, haricot beans, broken spaghetti or vermicelli, stale white bread, pepper, and saffron.

PRALINE PASTE ....

12 tablespoons castor sugar
4 tablespoons water
8 tablespoons in total of almonds and hazelnuts, pounded
Heat the sugar and water, stirring until the sugar is dissolved and comes to the boil. Then allow to boil without stirring until the syrup begins to color. The darker the color, the stronger the flavor, so stop the heat when it is light to avoid bitterness. Pour into a greased tray, or the mortar if it is heatproof, and cool the syrup for 1 hour until it sets hard. Break and pound with the nuts. The traditional praline is a smooth paste, but you can leave the nuts and caramel rough and textured if you choose. Ratio of sugar to nuts is 3:2.

QUENELLE PASTE ....

Quenelles are French delicate mini dumplings, usually made from finely ground fish or chicken. They are poached and then served with a sauce.

For 18-24 chicken quenelles:

1. Cut raw, boneless, chicken breasts from one chicken into small pieces and then grind in the mortar until the flesh has turned to a smooth paste. Add 1 tablespoon grated parmesan cheese, a grating of nutmeg, 1 egg, ½ cup thick cream, pepper, salt.
2. An alternate recipe is 500 grams soft chicken flesh, ground to a paste with 1 teaspoon salt, 1 teaspoon white pepper, 1 egg white, and 1 cup thick cream; push through a sieve if necessary.

Refrigerate mixture for an hour before poaching in a pot of gently simmering water or stock. Either mold the mixture into pointed rounds using 2 teaspoons and then use 1 teaspoon to push the mixture from the other teaspoon into the stock, or use a pastry bag fitted with a wide ½- to ¾-inch pastry nozzle, squeezing and cutting and dropping quenelles at ½-inch intervals into the stock. Gently simmer until the quenelles float to the surface or for 2-3 minutes. They will dry out if overcooked and disintegrate if the poaching liquid is on a rolling boil. Drain and serve immediately with a delicate sauce. If you are making in advance, they can be reheated with steam or by briefly simmering in water again. A fine flaked white fish can be substituted for the chicken or confit duck leg or thigh. Shallot, tarragon, mint, dill, and various aromatics and herbs can also be added.

RAS EL HANOUT SPICE ....
Ras el Hanout literally means "top or best of the shop" and represents the pinnacle of the Moroccan souk's (spice seller's) talent using his most precious and expensive ingredients. Sold as an aphrodisiac since antiquity, there are hundreds of recipes, as

each spice dealer has sought to outdo the other and woo the most prestigious customers. As with alchemy there are often eight base notes, which usually include allspice, black pepper, cinnamon, cardamom, clove, ginger, mace, and nutmeg. To these basics can be added a wide range of herbs and spices.

Make the base mix first:

¼ teaspoon ground allspice

1 teaspoon black peppercorns

1 teaspoon ground cinnamon

¼ teaspoon cardamom seeds, pods removed

3 cloves

1 teaspoon ground ginger

¼ teaspoon mace

¼ teaspoon ground nutmeg

••

For Recipe 1, add the following to the base mix.

1 teaspoon cumin seeds

1 teaspoon coriander seeds

¼ teaspoon ground turmeric

¼ teaspoon hot paprika

¼ teaspoon pink salt flakes

This will make approx 5 tablespoons of this complex North African herb and spice mix. The older recipes blend some twenty-five to thirty spices and herbs but remain a secret and much-coveted art. Ras el hanout is traditionally used with chicken, red meat, rice, and couscous but can be added to any savory dish.

••

For Recipe 2, add the following to the base mix.

2 teaspoons coriander seeds

2 teaspoons cumin

2 teaspoons turmeric

½ teaspoon saffron threads

½ teaspoon cayenne

½ teaspoon galangal

¼ teaspoon ajowan seeds (use parsley or fennel seeds as a substitute)

¼ teaspoon ambrette seeds (optional, because these musky sweet seeds have no close substitue)

1 teaspoon each of small rose and lavender buds

REMPAH ....

This spicy paste has many forms and is used widely in Malay, Nyonya, and Asian cuisines as a base for fish, meat, and vegetable curries. Once fried, coconut milk can also be added. There are many optional ingredients that can be added to make the flavor more complex.

2 long red and/or green chilies

4—6 garlic cloves

Grated or finely chopped ginger, 2-inch piece

2 chopped pieces lemongrass

1 teaspoon turmeric powder

Salt, sugar to taste

Optional additions can include macadamia or brazil nuts, onions/shallots, shrimp paste, galangal, basil, and coriander.

RILLETTE ....

Rillette is a country-style pate or spiced meat paste with a soft, smooth texture. Traditionally it is made from cubed pork belly, goose, duck, or chicken meat that is salted, cured, and slowly cooked in fat. It can also be made from fresh or canned tuna or anchovies and raw salmon or any smoked fish.

250 grams fish, pork, duck, chicken, or goose

5 tablespoons unsalted soft butter

2 tablespoons fresh herbs, e.g., chives, parsley, tarragon, fennel, or sage

Lemon juice to taste

Salt if required

Optional spices such as paprika, nutmeg, or chili can be added.

Grind until smooth and soft, and spread on hot toasts or canapés.

SAFFRON PASTE ....

6-8 saffron strands soaked in 2 tablespoons boiling water

2 tablespoons tahini

2 garlic cloves

2 tablespoons olive oil

2 tablespoons lemon juice

1 tablespoon fresh mint leaves

1 tablespoon fresh thyme leaves

Salt/pepper

Mix all together to a smooth paste and add vegetable stock until it reaches the consistency you like. This can be served drizzled over grilled or roast vegetables and meats or as a dip for raw vegetables.

SAMBAL PASTE (DIMMY'S CHILI PASTE) ....

15 garlic cloves

1 ripe tomato, chopped

12 small (about 1-inch-long hot) or 6 large (4- to 5-inch-long) red chilies, with seeds

Grind to a paste. Before use, heat ¼ cup vegetable oil in a small saucepan, add the paste, and fry until the oil begins to rise to the surface. Store in the fridge.

Option 2: You can add a teaspoon of fish sauce and a teaspoon of shrimp paste or dried shrimp to the grind before frying off.

Serve with chicken or fish as a sauce on the side or spread over the food as it cooks.

THAI GREEN CURRY PASTE (KHREUANG KAENG KHIAWWAAN) ....

8 small green seeded chilies (2 inches each), roughly chopped

2 lemongrass stalks, chopped white part only

1 lime, zested, or its finely sliced skin

4 garlic cloves

3 shallots

4 holy basil sets, including stems (½ cup)

2 teaspoons shrimp paste

1 teaspoon coriander seeds, dry roasted

1 teaspoon brown sugar or palm sugar

Salt

Oil to wet paste

THAI RED CURRY PASTE (KHREUANG KAENG PHET) ....

3 long red seeded chilies, roughly chopped; if using dried chilies, reconstitute in hot water for a couple of minutes before chopping
8 small red seeded chilies, as above
2 lemongrass stalks, chopped white part only
Golf-ball-sized piece of galangal, chopped
1 lime, zested or finely sliced skin
4 garlic cloves
4 shallots
4 coriander sets (stalks, usually 3 or 4, joined at the root), including stems and roots, approximately ½ cup
2 teaspoons shrimp paste
1 teaspoon coriander seeds, dry roasted
1 teaspoon brown sugar or palm sugar
Salt
Oil to wet the paste

THAI YELLOW CURRY PASTE (KHREUANG KAENG LEUANG) ....

3 long red seeded chilies (5 inches each), roughly chopped
2 lemongrass stalks, chopped white part only
2 garlic cloves
3 shallots
1 teaspoon shrimp paste
3 teaspoons coriander seeds, dry roasted
1 teaspoon cumin seeds, dry roasted
1 teaspoon turmeric
1 teaspoon brown sugar or palm sugar
Salt
Oil to wet paste

WALNUT SAUCE ....

3 garlic cloves
2 teaspoons smoked ground paprika
Salt/pepper
2 finely chopped shallots or 1 finely chopped small onion
2 chopped, fresh, white bread slices, with crusts
2 tablespoons oil
1 cup walnut meat, ground in last, either to a fine paste or coarse if you like texture.
When mixed together, transfer to a small saucepan and heat in 2 tablespoons butter until the mixture is cooked to a golden color. Then add 500 milliliters of chicken stock and stir to a slow boil. Reduce to the consistency you like and taste for seasoning. In Mediterranean countries, this sauce is served as an accompaniment to meat, chicken, pasta, or fish, and a few extra toasted walnut pieces are added at the last minute before serving hot. The flavor is delicious and rich, and if you prefer, a few tablespoons of cream can be added at the last minute for added silkiness, or a few fresh green herbs, like tarragon, thyme, or oregano.

ZAATAR SPICE MIX ....

2 tablespoons sesame seeds, dry roasted until just colored
2 tablespoons dried oregano
1 tablespoon dried thyme
1 tablespoon ground sumac*
Sumac, along with lemon and pomegranate, defines the Middle Eastern love affair with sour flavors. It has a tangy lemon flavor and is the ground, dried, dark red berry of the wonderful sumac shrub, available in gourmet grocers and Middle Eastern and African grocers and spice markets. Widely cultivated in Lebanon and Syria, sumac is also a favorite spice in Iran, Iraq, and Turkey.

In Morocco, North Africa, Greece, Turkey, and Jordan, zaatar is used as a food sprinkle, a marinade, and a dipping spice for bread with olive oil, or added to dishes as a spice. Once you've made this, it's easy to see why this ancient recipe has been in daily continual use for thousands of years.

MARINADES

*"The love of food marinades the heart to make both
more tender"*
—THE CULINARY LIBRARY

A marinade is a seasoned liquid, paste, or dry mixture, either cooked or uncooked, in which other foods are steeped in order to merge flavors and soften fibers. Marinades are a quick and easy way to intensify flavor, tenderize, and moisten foods, especially raw meats. A marinade can also be used and served as a pickling agent, as with mushrooms, cherries, oysters, or carpaccio beef or fish. From the Latin *mare*, meaning "sea," or *mar*, meaning "bitter," and *marina*, meaning "briny," marinades were originally used to pickle fish in a salty, bitter brine water.

The Greco Romans made a fish marinade of fermented anchovies, called *garum*, which was a large part of their staple daily diet. They extended this to using salt as a dry rub and a brine to marinate pork and meats, and barreled them for use on long sea journeys and war campaigns.

Pre-Colombian Mexicans and South Sea islanders used papaya leaves and fruit (the enzyme papain) to tenderize their meat before and during cooking.

More than three thousand years ago, the Chinese were using the fermented sauce of the soybean as a tenderizing marinade.

The first bottled marinade sauce commercially available appears to have been made in the United States of America in the early 1800s, when a banker, Mr. Edward McIlhenny, on retiring from the Civil War to his farm on Avery Island in Louisiana, planted two acres of a chili variety called Tabasco, and the rest is history.

In the 1830s in the United Kingdom, it is thought that a Mrs. Grey, niece to Sir Charles Grey, gave her friend Mary a marinade recipe that her uncle had found whilst he was chief justice of India. Mary Sandys Hill was the mother of Lord Arthur Moyses William Sandys, 1792-1860, lieutenant general, member of the House of Commons, and the second Baron Sandys of Worcestershire. Some of the ingredients would have been beyond their knowledge, such as the tamarind extract and soy sauce, so it is believed either Mary or her son commissioned the two local dispensing chemists to make a first facsimile batch of marinade. Mr. John Wheeley Lea and Mr. William Henry Perrins did their best, and Messrs. Lea & Perrins' Worcestershire sauce and marinade became commercially available from 1837. It is still in commercial production some 173 years later, although bought by H. J. Heinz Company in 2005.

Today marinades can be liquid, dry, or paste and are used for vegetables and fruits as well as fish and meats.

Marinades are usually, but not always, made up of three substances:

1. FAT: Oil locks in moisture and either adds or carries flavor; e.g., olive, sesame, peanut, and infused oils.
2. ACID: Acid tenderizes by unraveling the proteins that bind the food particles together. This process is called denaturing the protein and it makes the surface tension

of food relax, making it softer, more digestible and more pervious so flavor can be absorbed. Acids include vinegar, wine, sherry, citrus, papaya, pomegranate juice, and yogurt.

3. FLAVOR ADDITIVES: The third ingredients are seasonings that add additional flavors, such as garlic, ginger, onion, herbs, chili, honey, sugar, peels, soy, mustard, salt, and spices.

In general, the following rules apply when using marinades:

— The lighter the color of the food, the shorter the time needed to marinate. Fish, for example, can literally "cook" in the acid of lemon juice in minutes, and shaved strips of cucumber or white radish will need even less. (If you have ever left salad dressed in a marinade of dressing overnight you, will be aware that its molecular bonds break down so much that the salad is slimy and no longer edible.)

— The thicker and tougher the food, the longer you will need to marinate.

— All food sitting in a marinade is best stored in the fridge, especially meat, and especially overnight. Do not be fooled into assuming acid will kill bacteria.

— The acid in marinades reacts with some metals and dissolves them, so do not marinate in aluminum foil or reactive metals. I find the easiest, safest, and cleanest method is to use a zip-top plastic bag, which can be turned and squished regularly to coat the food.

— Marinades must boil to kill bacteria.

Try using the marinades listed below and modify as you go, or, better still, invent new ones.

AUSSIE BBQ MARINADE ....

2 garlic cloves, ½ chopped onion, 3 tablespoons Worcestershire sauce, 3 tablespoons tomato sauce, 2 tablespoons soy sauce, 1 tablespoon Dijon mustard, 3 tablespoons parsley, 3 tablespoons balsamic vinegar, salt, pepper and ½ cup beer.

BALSAMIC MARINADE ....

2 garlic cloves, 1 cup balsamic vinegar, ½ cup brown sugar or honey, 1 tablespoon Dijon mustard, pepper, olive oil.

BASIC WINE MARINADE (UNCOOKED) ....

Grind ½ diced onion, ½ diced carrot, 1 stick diced celery, 2   garlic cloves, one tablespoon each of fresh parsley and thyme, 1 bay leaf, peppercorns to taste, 1 clove, and salt. Moisten with ½ cup of oil. Remove from the mortar to a large zip-top bag and add 1 cup of red or white wine. Immerse meat, seafood, or vegetables and seal. Gently coat food with the marinade and set aside in the fridge until use, overnight if possible. A little lemon juice, brandy, and other herbs can be added or substituted. The marinade can also be cooked prior to immersion of the meat.

BUTTER CHICKEN MARINADE ....

2 garlic cloves, 1 tablespoon gingerroot, 1 teaspoon red chilies, 1 teaspoon turmeric, 1 teaspoon paprika, 1 teaspoon cumin, 1 teaspoon coriander, juice of 1 lemon, 1 teaspoon fish sauce. Makes enough to coat 1 raw chicken breast or 2 thighs. Marinate in zip-top bag overnight in fridge. Cook both the chicken and marinade in a hot well oiled pan for a few minutes, then add a little coconut milk and simmer gently. Serve with fresh coriander and mint.

CARPACCIO BEEF MARINADE ....

½ red onion, chopped, 1 teaspoon Dijon mustard, 2 tablespoon cider or white wine vinegar, 4 tablespoons olive oil, fresh rosemary, parsley, or tarragon.

Arrange paper-thin slices of raw fillet steak in a circular fan shape around a plate, drizzle with the marinade, and chill.

Can decorate with edible flowers and baby leaves, e.g., baby nasturtium and tiny inner leaves of frizzy endive.

CARPACCIO SWORDFISH, TUNA, OR SCALLOP MARINADE ....

Gently grind together fresh thyme, chervil, a small amount of chopped red chili, white or pink peppercorns, 2 tablespoons lemon juice, 4 tablespoons olive oil.

Arrange paper-thin slices of raw seafood to cover a plate, drizzle with the marinade and pink flaked salt, and allow the acid to "cook" the flesh. Decorate with edible flowers if you have some in your garden, e.g., blue borage or those wonderfully delicate mustard rocket flowers. Chilling the seafood in the freezer makes the slicing easier and more even. Bring to room temperature before serving.

CHICKEN TIKKA MARINADE ....

2 teaspoons garlic, 2 teaspoons ginger, 2 teaspoons coriander seeds, 1 teaspoon cumin seeds, 2 teaspoons Kashmiri curry powder, ½ teaspoon Punjab garam masala, ½ teaspoon turmeric, ½ teaspoon mace, ½ cup plain yogurt. Marinate chicken thighs or breast in zip-top bag overnight in fridge. Cook chicken and marinade in a hot oiled pan for a few minutes, then add a little coconut milk and simmer gently. Serve with fresh coriander and mint.

CHINESE MARINADE ....

1 tablespoon sugar, 2 tablespoons soy sauce, 1 tablespoon hoisin sauce, 1 tablespoon crunchy peanut paste (peanut butter), 1 tablespoon black bean sauce, ½ cup Chinese cooking wine, salt.

CUBAN MARINADE ....

5 garlic cloves, small chopped onion, 1 teaspoon oregano, 2 tablespoons parsley, salt, pepper, juice of an orange, juice of a lime, 1 cup oil.

EGYPTIAN MARINADE ....

¼ onion, 2-3 garlic cloves, 1 teaspoon cayenne pepper, salt, black pepper, 3 tablespoons coriander seeds, 2 tablespoons cumin seeds, ¾ cup oil.

A recipe from the New Kingdom of Ancient Egypt, used for duck, goose, and chicken.

FISH MARINADE 1 ....

2 garlic cloves, 1 teaspoon thyme, 1 teaspoon oregano, juice of 1 lemon, 1 tablespoon olive oil, ½ teaspoon sweet smoked paprika, salt, pepper.

FISH MARINADE 2 ....

2 garlic cloves, 1 teaspoon cumin seeds, juice of 1 lemon, 1 tablespoon olive oil, 1 tablespoon lemon myrtle, salt, pepper.

GARLIC MARINADE ....

1 tablespoon Dijon mustard, 3 garlic cloves, 1 teaspoon basil, 1 teaspoon coriander, 2 tablespoons white wine, 2 tablespoons lemon

or lime juice, ½ cup oil, ½ cup fresh oregano, zest and juice of 1 lemon, salt, pepper, ⅔ cup olive oil.
Great for prawns or red meat.

LAMB MARINADE ....

2 garlic cloves, 2 teaspoons fresh thyme, 2 teaspoons parsley, 1 teaspoon sweet smoked paprika, 1 tablespoon olive oil, 2 table-spoons red wine vinegar or juice of 1 lemon, salt, pepper.

MOUNTAIN PEPPER MARINADE ....

12 large black mountain peppercorns (Australian)
12 black peppercorns
12 pink or red peppercorns
12 green peppercorns
Salt
Crack and grind all together, then add ½ cup oil. Use half to coat fillet steaks then cook them on a high heat in a well-buttered/oiled pan on top of the stove. Remove steaks when medium rare to a serving platter and rest in the oven on 150°C/300°F, for a few minutes. While steaks are resting, add the remaining marinade to the pan and heat, then deglaze the pan with a splash of cognac or brandy. Tilt the pan to burn off the alcohol if using a gas stove, or put a match to it otherwise. Add 1 cup of cream and bring to a boil. Stir the pan and wait for the sauce to begin thickening and just starting to deepen in color. Serve hot over the steak.

MOROCCAN MARINADE ....

½ onion, 4 garlic cloves, ½ teaspoon turmeric, 3 tablespoons cumin, 2 teaspoons paprika, 1 bay leaf, juice of 1 lemon, coriander (fresh or seeds), ½ cup oil.

PAPAYA MARINADE ....

1 peeled, deseeded and chopped papaya, 1 tablespoon soy sauce, 2 tablespoons sugar, salt, pepper. Good for tenderizing meat.

PINEAPPLE MARINADE 1 ....

1 cup crushed pineapple pieces, 2 tablespoons mint leaves, 3 tablespoons light brown sugar, 2 tablespoons dark rum, 1 teaspoon vanilla, ⅓ cup boiling water.
Use for dessert fruits or marinating meat.

PINEAPPLE MARINADE 2 ....

½ cup crushed pineapple, 2 tablespoons soy, 2 tablespoons honey, 2 garlic cloves, 2 teaspoons ginger, 1 clove, and 4 tablespoons cider vinegar.

POMEGRANATE MARINADE ....

2 garlic cloves, ½ red onion, 2 tablespoons balsamic vinegar, 4 tablespoons pomegranate syrup or 2 tablespoons pomegranate molasses, ½ cup oil.

SPARERIB MARINADE ....

3 tablespoons honey, 2 tablespoons soy sauce, 1 tablespoon oyster sauce, 1 tablespoon light brown sugar, 1 tablespoon fresh ginger, 3 garlic cloves, 2 tablespoons tomato paste, 2 tablespoons lemon or orange juice, pinch cayenne pepper, pinch cinnamon, pinch rosemary, salt.

SPICY PLUM MARINADE ....

½ onion, 2 garlic cloves, 1 teaspoon five spice powder, 2 plums whole or chopped but destoned, 1 tablespoon light brown sugar, 4 tablespoons vinegar. If you do not have fresh plums, replace the last 3 ingredients with ½ cup plum sauce.

STEAK MARINADE ....

2 tablespoons thyme, 6 garlic cloves, 2 tablespoons olive oil, ½ cup red wine.

TERIYAKI MARINADE ....

2 garlic cloves, 3 tablespoons ginger, 3 tablespoons spring onion, 2 tablespoons five spice powder, ½ cup light brown sugar or honey, ¼ cup rice wine or semi-dry sherry, 1 cup soy sauce.

THAI MARINADE ....

2 tablespoons sugar, 1 tablespoon peanut oil, 1 tablespoon fish sauce, 2 tablespoons sweet chili sauce, 2 tablespoons lime juice, ½ cup fresh coriander including leaves, clean roots, and stalks. Use for chicken, fish, and lamb.

COMPOUND BUTTERS

"Butter is.......the most delicate of foods among barbarous nations, and one which distinguishes the wealthy from the multitude at large."
—PLINY

A compound butter is a butter mixed with one or more other substances to infuse flavor. Usually solid butter is softened to room temperature and then pounded until it is light and creamy in texture before the additives are mixed in. Occasionally butter is melted and cooked to varying degrees, then resolidified. Once compounded, the butter can be placed on cling film or foil, rolled into a log shape, and frozen or refrigerated; scooped soft into a piping bag for use on canapés, hard-boiled eggs, decoration, etc.; used as a spread; or molded or cut into shapes. More usually, it is set aside in the fridge or freezer to reharden for future use. Lozenge-size rounds are cut from the log and are available as a supplement to sauces and cooked dishes or as a garnish.

Compound butters are also known as beurre compose, finishing butters, or flavored butters. Their exact origin is unknown, but compound butters were probably invented in France in the late 1700s in the time of the first celebrity chef, Marie-Antoine Careme, or his predecessor, Savart.

The ancient Greeks and Romans thought the use of butter barbaric, and if they wanted to insult someone, like the Thracians, they called them "butter eaters." By the twelfth century, the Scandinavians were making and exporting butter as cheap peasant food, and it became popular at that time because the Roman Catholic Church said it could be eaten during Lent.

By the 1860s in France, butter had supplanted lard as the domesticated fat of choice in French cooking, and when Normandy and Brittany could not supply enough to meet demand, Napoleon III was forced to offer a substantial prize to anyone who could invent a cheap, imitation as a substitute. A French chemist won the prize in 1869 when he successfully emulsified beef tallow and milk and called it "margarine." The name "margarine" was later taken over by the inventors of hydrogenated vegetable oil in 1900. Today's margarines are highly processed, may contain anything up to 50 percent trans fats, and to us taste synthetic and bland. After a quick dabble in the nineties with the ones we were falsely led to believe were "healthy," we have abandoned them totally and cannot recommend them. If you are committed to only using margarine and are not prepared to use butter, we suggest you skip this section altogether.

Also, in the midseventeenth century, the traditional thickeners of bread, rice, and almond meal were replaced by the innovation of mixing flour into butter. This was, and still is, called "roux," and this was the first widely used compound butter and is still the basis of many French sauces.

But Careme specialized in inventing soups and grand patisserie work (he made Napoleon's wedding cake), so it is from his successor, Auguste Escoffier, writing in the 1930s that we get our first comprehensive recipes when, in his book *Le Guide Culinaire*, he lists thirty-five different compound butters.

As well as experimenting with compound butters, it is necessary to be aware that the type of butter you choose will affect the flavor. The various types of butter you can choose from are as follows, and most come in both salted and unsalted forms:

1. Raw Cream Butter: Also called farm butter, it is made by churning the cream extracted from whole, unpasteurized cow's milk. It has a fresh, clean, uncooked flavor, and its color varies depending on the time of year the milk is collected and the feed available to the cows. With spring grass, the color will be slightly darker and the flavor stronger compared to the dry feeding of cows in the winter.

2. Sweet Cream Butter: Made by churning the cream extracted from whole, pasteurized cow's milk. This type of butter is popular in the United States, United Kingdom, and Australia. It has a sweet, soft flavor on the palate.

3. Cultured Butter: Made by churning the cream extracted from whole, naturally fermented and aged cow's milk. This type of butter is popular in Europe and is also known as European butter. Traditionally made using naturally soured whole milk, it has a rich, more intense, and slightly sour flavor.

4. Clarified Butter: Butter that is heated to the 100°C/212°F melting point, cooled, and skimmed of its whey protein. With the water and milk solids removed, it is almost pure butterfat.

5. Ghee: Clarified butter that is heated further to approximately 120°C/250°F. This cooks to a light brown the milk solids (protein and casein), which are removed after evaporating the water. The fat left behind is called ghee. Because of being heated to a high temperature, it has a

longer shelf life of approximately six to eight months, a high smoke point, and, unlike normal butter, it does not splatter when used for frying. Ghee is popular in India, called samna in Egypt and sman in Africa.

6. Whey Butter: Salty, tangy, and cheesy in flavor with a lower fat content.
7. Goat Butter: It has a sweet, creamy flavor, but is a specialty food item.
8. Ewe Milk Fats: Used for butter and found mainly in Egyptian samna.
9. Buffalo Milk Fats: Used for butter and found mainly in Indian ghee.

Most commercial mass-produced butter is made from minute amounts of cream reclaimed and extracted by centrifugal force from the by-product whey of the cheese-making process. It is usually saltier and its flavors simulated by adding lactic acid, bacteria, and artificial flavor and color enhancers.

Spreadable butters are made spreadable by chemical manipulation and often the incorporation of vegetable oil.

Whipped butter is aerated with nitrogen gas to make it light and fluffy.

Margarine is not butter.

All recipes below are for use with 250 grams of softened, unsalted butter (approximately thirty one-inch-lozenge-sized servings.) If this is too much for you, use half the butter and, where recipes have ingredient amounts listed, halve these as well. We have purposefully left the measure and balance of additive ingredients to your own taste buds, except where the recipe is more complex, well known, or traditional. It is recommended you mix the flavor additives together first and incorporate the butter last. Taste and adjust additives. Incorporate salt if necessary at the end. Don't worry if you get the flavor balances wrong a few times to begin with, as continual tasting is still the best way to train your palate to know what flavors you like rather than robotically accepting someone else's ideas.

ALMOND BUTTER ....
8 tablespoons ground almond meal, 1 tablespoon water. Great on cake, croissants, toast, vegetables.

ANCHOVY BUTTER ....
This was a popular favorite in London from the 1700s right through the roaring 1920s until falling from mass consumption around the '50s and '60s. Fortnum & Mason's London sold, and probably still does sell, beautiful ceramic pots of this spread, which it called gentleman's relish. Certainly it was popular in the Georgian era, when Joseph Bank's cook, Mr. Henry Osborne, used to prepare it for Sir Joseph and his friends in his Soho Square

house in London in the late 1700s. Simply bone and lightly wipe down as many anchovies as suit your taste, grind them with the butter in a mortar and pestle until soft and creamy, and adjust the taste to your preference by the addition of one or several of the following: lemon juice, pepper, mustard or curry powder, cayenne or mace. Traditionally served either on toast that was very hot or spread on bread that was then lightly fried, this is also great with steak and seriously underrated.

BLACK GARLIC BUTTER ....

Black garlic is garlic that has undergone a long fermentation process under controlled heat. It has a sweet, rich, jellylike taste and feel. Compounded with butter, it adds an interesting kick to steak, seafood, and pasta.

BLUE CHEESE OR ROQUEFORT BUTTER ....

8 ounces or approximately 250 grams of Roquefort cheese, crumbled, 2 teaspoons minced garlic, 4 teaspoons fresh chopped chive, 4 teaspoons fresh chopped thyme or parsley, ground black pepper to taste.

As there is an equal amount of cheese to butter in this recipe, it makes a large quantity which is great for a party or bbq. Halve or quarter the ingredients for home use if you prefer.

Once mixed to a smooth paste, this delicious compound butter can be served on top of hot sizzling steaks, buttered onto toast, melted onto bruschetta, in pasta or over vegetables. What ever you do though, do not try this on crunchy roast potatoes unless you need a new food addiction.

CAFÉ DE PARIS BUTTER ....

This famous butter was invented in France by Freddy Dumont in 1941 and was traditionally served on top of porterhouse or sirloin steak and served with pommes frites or chips. The original method called for the butter to be melted and the rest of the ingredients made to a paste, infused overnight, then added to the butter, reset, and rolled, ready for the freezer. I soften my butter in the mortar, then add the ingredients a few at a time.

1½ tablespoons tomato sauce or ketchup, 1 teaspoon Dijon mustard, 1 teaspoon small capers, 1 shallot or ½ teaspoon onion, 1 tablespoon fresh chopped parsley, 1 tablespoon fresh chopped chives, 1 tablespoon fresh chopped French tarragon, 1 teaspoon fresh chopped marjoram, 1 teaspoon fresh chopped dill, 1 teaspoon fresh chopped thyme, ½ teaspoon fresh chopped rosemary, 1 garlic clove, 2 anchovies, 1 teaspoon brandy, 1 teaspoon Madeira, ¼ teaspoon Worcestershire sauce, ¼ teaspoon sweet paprika, ¼ teaspoon curry powder, 1 tablespoon lemon zest, 1 tablespoon orange zest, pepper, salt.

CAPER TARRAGON BUTTER ....

2 cups fresh tarragon leaves, no stems
½ cup capers
zest and juice from 1 lemon
salt and white or black pepper to taste
Excellent used under the skin of chicken, turkey and ducks before roasting. Also good with fish and puttanesca pasta. For variety you can also add add ½ to one teaspoons of smoked paprika.

CAVIAR BUTTER ....
4 tablespoons caviar. Serve with canapés, fish, seafood, and crustaceans.

CHAMPAGNE BUTTER ....
2 cups of pink champagne reduced to ¼ of original volume, seeds from 1-2 vanilla pods or ½ teaspoon extract, 1 tablespoon chervil or tarragon. Pink and green peppercorns left whole and added at the end are optional. Try and get the fresh vanilla, as the black seeds and green of the herb look great suspended and dispersing in a light consommé or flavored broth. Serve with poached chicken, white fish, fresh steamed artichoke hearts, or white asparagus. Serve also with seafood and crustaceans.

CHARDONNAY AND SAGE BUTTER ....
Reduce 2 cups of chardonnay to ¼ of original volume and add to ground butter with ½ cup fresh sage leaves or 1 cup lightly fried sage leaves, salt and pepper.

CHILI LIME BUTTER ....
4 tablespoons long red and/or green chilies, seeded, 2 tablespoons lime zest, 2 tablespoons lime juice. Use wild limes if you have them.

CHOCOLATE HAZELNUT BUTTER ....
8 tablespoons ground hazelnuts, 4 tablespoons melted or grated dark chocolate.

CHOCOLATE ORANGE JAFFA BUTTER ....
½ cup dark bitter-sweet (70%+ cocoa) chocolate, chopped, melted and cooled, 1 tablespoons cocoa powder, 2 tablespoons grated orange zest, 2 tablespoons powdered /confectioners sugar

CHOCOLATE WHITE BUTTER ....
½ cup white chocolate, chopped, melted and cooled, 1 level teaspoon ground cinnamon. Try this spread on pancakes, scones, toast, warm brioche or toasted panettone.

CRANBERRY SAGE BUTTER ....
½ cup fresh sage leaves or 1 cup lightly fried sage leaves, 1 clove garlic, 1 cup cranberries or thick cranberry sauce, salt and pepper. Excellent for Thanksgiving or Christmas celebrations.

CREPES SUZETTE BUTTER ....
4-6 tablespoons orange, mandarin, or tangerine zest, 2 tablespoons juice from same, 4 tablespoons powdered or icing sugar; 2 tablespoons white Curacao is optional. Spread on warm crepes, then fold into quarters and reheat in the pan or oven with orange juice or syrup to moisten. Dust with powdered sugar. Crepes can be spread and folded the day before being used but need to be reheated longer until the compound butter melts. Flame with spirits if desired. You can also add a little maple syrup to this compound butter and spread on hot waffles.

CURRY ORANGE BUTTER ....
One onion sweated until soft and golden in oil and butter, 1 tablespoon of curry powder added and cooked. Add to the butter in the mortar and pestle with 1 garlic clove, 1 tablespoon of orange

zest, 1 tablespoon chopped parsley, capers, basil, thyme, ginger, anchovy, lemon, Worcestershire, salt, pepper.

EGG YOLK BUTTER ....

4 hard boiled egg yolks, 1 tablespoon Dijon mustard, 2 tablespoons mayonnaise, 1 teaspoon lemon juice or white wine vinegar, salt and white pepper to taste.

FIG ORANGE BUTTER ....

4 or 5 roughly chopped fresh figs or diced dried figs soaked until soft, zest and juice of 1 orange, pinch of cinnamon, 2 tablespoons castor or powdered sugar, 1 teaspoon vanilla extract or seeds from 1 vanilla pod.

GARLIC BUTTER ....

5 garlic cloves, 1 tablespoon grated parmesan cheese

GREEN TEA MATCHA BUTTER ....

Add as little or as much Matcha green tea powder to butter as you feel suits your palate. Salt, pepper and sugar can also be added to taste. Matcha is a very finely milled, high quality green tea used in the traditional Japanese tea ceremony. It has a wide range of culinary uses including flavouring confectionery, icecream, chocolate, caramel and creams.

HERB BUTTER ....

Spring onion or shallots, garlic, 2 tablespoons lemon juice, fresh soft herbs of your choice (e.g., parsley, tarragon, coriander, sage, chervil, chives, mint).

HONEY BUTTER ....
½ cup honey, cinnamon to taste.

HONEY ORANGE BUTTER ....
½ cup honey, cinnamon, 2 tablespoons orange, mandarin, or tangerine zest, and 2 tablespoons of the citrus juice.

HONEY PECAN BUTTER ....
½ cup honey, cinnamon, 1 cup pecan nuts.

HORSERADISH BUTTER ....
⅓ cup fresh grated horseradish or 2 tablespoons of preserved horseradish. Add a little cream if you want it softer.

KEY LIME BUTTER ....
Finely grated zest and juice of 2 limes, salt and pepper to taste

LAVENDER BUTTER ....
1 cup lavender flowers, 1 tablespoon honey, 1 tablespoon parsley or french tarragon, salt and pepper to taste. If you have access to other edible flowers a few can also be added eg yellow marigold petals added at the end compliment the lavender.

LEMON DILL BUTTER ....
Finely grated zest and juice of 2 lemons, 1 cup dill fronds, salt and pepper to taste.

LEMON MUSTARD BUTTER ....
Finely grated zest and juice of 1 lemon, 2 tablespoons prepared mustard of your choice, salt and pepper to taste.

LIQUEUR CHERRY BUTTER ....

2 cups of morello cherries or 1 cup of maraschino cherries, the red ones if you want almond flavor or the green ones if you want peppermint flavored butter.

MAITRE D'HOTEL BUTTER ....

½ cup chopped Italian leaf parsley, juice of 1 lemon, salt, pepper.

MAPLE SYRUP BUTTER ....

½ cup maple syrup, 2 teaspoons cinnamon, 1 tablespoon orange juice, 1 tablespoon rum.

MONTPELLIER BUTTER ....

2 garlic cloves, 2 shallots chopped, 4 anchovy fillets, ½ cup mixed herbs chopped like parsley, chervil, chives and tarragon, ½ cup chopped rocket, ½ cup cooked spinach, 1 tablespoon capers, 2 hard boiled egg yolks, 2 small chopped gherkins, 2 tablespoons olive oil, salt, pepper.

MUSHROOM BUTTER ....

Sauté roughly chopped mushrooms in butter in a pan until the moisture evaporates and they turn a golden honey brown. Cool and then add to the butter in the mortar and mix to a smooth paste. Season with pepper and test to see if salt is needed.

NUT BUTTERS ....

Nut butter usually refers to butter that has been heated to a light nut brown color. Here we mean incorporating the actual nuts into the butter. Use your favorite nuts—walnut, pecan, almond, macadamia, hazel, Brazil, pine, peanut—with garlic, salt/pepper, mustard for savory butter, or orange or lemon or lime zest and sugar for sweet butter.

ORANGE MINT BUTTER ....
Fresh small mint leaves, 1 tablespoon castor or powdered sugar, 2 tablespoons orange, mandarin, or tangerine zest, and 2 tablespoons juice. Replace the mint with some grated chocolate to make Jaffa butter.

PECAN MAPLE SYRUP BUTTER ....
4-8 tablespoons pecan meat, 4 tablespoons maple syrup.

PESTO BUTTER ....
Basil leaves, pine nuts and/or walnuts, garlic, salt, pepper.

PINA COLADA BUTTER ....
8 tablespoons canned crushed pineapple, drained, 1 cup flaked coconut, and maraschino cherries to taste, chopped, drained.

PINE NUT BUTTER ....
1 cup pine nuts, 1 cup parsley, ½ cup parmesan, pepper and salt to taste

POMEGRANATE ORANGE BUTTER ....
2 tablespoons pomegranate molasses, 2 tablespoons orange zest, 1 tablespoon confectioners or powdered sugar or more to taste, ¼ cup chopped nuts of your choice.

PRINTANIER BUTTER ....
To the warmed creamed butter, add a mixture of cooked vegetables and grind until smooth. Vegetables can include any in season,

e.g., carrot, turnip, parsnip, pumpkin, beans, peas, asparagus, artichoke, etc. An old French compound butter used as a garnish for hot soup or meat entrees that are served with baby vegetables. It is usually balled with a melon baler or cut into small dice and placed on top of the food at the time of serving. It is a good way to use up leftover roasted vegetables and roasting fats that impart an even richer flavor to the butter. After making the butter, let it cool down before balling or dicing it, or freeze as normal in a rolled log and slice off thin lozenges to float on hot soup.

RED WINE BUTTER ....
Reduce 2 cups of good red wine with some chopped shallots over heat to ¼ of its original volume. Add lemon zest and a little juice and chopped parsley. Place in the mortar and work in the butter and flaked salt.

ROUX ....
Beurre manie or roux is made by creaming butter with the pestle and then mixing in an equal part of plain flour and grinding to a smooth paste. This can be added as a thickener to hot foods or cooked over heat before adding stock or milk to begin a sauce.

SAFFRON BUTTER ....
Infuse a large pinch of saffron threads in 1 teaspoon of warm champagne vinegar or apple cider and mix with the creamed butter. Season with salt and pepper to taste.

SAUTERNE BUTTER ....
Reduce your favorite sauterne or sweet white wine over heat to ¼ of its original volume. Add orange zest and a little juice, and

a sprinkle of cane, castor, or powdered sugar. Add parsley, tarragon, sage, or chervil.

SMOKED PAPRIKA ....
2 tablespoons smoked paprika, salt.

SNAIL BUTTER OR BEURRE D'ESCARGOT ....
½ shallot, 2 garlic cloves, 2 tablespoons parsley, salt, pepper. Traditionally served with snails in the shell.

SOUR CHERRY BUTTER ....
1 cup pitted fresh or bottled cherries, 1 tablespoon balsamic or cider vinegar, 1 tablespoon castor or powdered sugar, 1 tablespoon orange zest, 1 teaspoon pomegranate powder or pomegranate molasses. Serve with red meat, poultry, and game, or hot fruit desserts. Other red fruits can be substituted in season, such as cranberries, red currants, or pomegranate arils(seeds).

SPICED RUM AND RAISIN BUTTER ....
2 or three tablespoons of raisins soaked in 5 tablespoons of rum, 1 teaspoon of pure vanilla extract or 1 fresh chopped vanilla pod with seeds and powdered sugar to taste.

TARRAGON BUTTER ....
1-2 cups fresh tarragon leaves, salt, pepper.

TRUFFLE BUTTER ....
As much chopped fresh truffle as you can afford.

TUSCAN HERB BUTTER ....
Basil, parsley, rosemary, thyme, garlic.

WALNUT BUTTER ....
2 cups walnuts, 1 teaspoon cinnamon, 1 teaspoon powdered sugar, 1 teaspoon of lemon or lime juice, 1 pinch of finishing salt. This can be used for both sweet and savoury dishes.

WALNUT RAISIN BUTTER ....
1 cup walnuts, ½ cup raisins soaked for a couple of hours or overnight in brandy, port, or muscat, cinnamon, nutmeg, mace, 2 tablespoons honey. Fantastic on waffles, pancakes, roast pork, venison, chicken, and game birds. You can also mix this in a hot toddy or egg nog.

WASABI BUTTER ....
1-2 tablespoons wasabi.

WHISKEY BUTTER ....
4-8 tablespoons whiskey or cognac, powdered sugar to taste.

AETHEROLEA

———•◆•———

"And he made the holy anointing oil, and the pure incense of sweet spices, according to the work of the apothecary."
—THE BIBLE

DEFINITION ....
We've used the descriptor "Aetherolea" to describe these heavenly flavor-infused culinary oils. Aetherolea means simply a water-resistant (hydrophobic) liquid that contains volatile aroma compounds from plants. Because they are made in such small quantities, the mortar and pestle are perfect for making these delicate drops. By grinding out the flavor and aroma compounds from plants and mixing them with a carrier, a food additive is produced that will convey visual appeal, fragrance, and color to a finished dish. The field of aromatherapy believes specific aromas or essential oils have curative effects; however, the edible atherolea described here are essence oils and should not be confused with their cousins, the essential oil concentrates which are primarily for external use only. Because we are using neither distillation nor solvents to extract the flavor from plants but rather the friction and gentle heat of the mortar and pestle, aetherolea are edible provided you do not use toxic plants or seeds.

Aroma and flavor molecule compounds in plants and food are extremely volatile, especially under heat. This means they readily vaporize. Your nose knows this automatically when you enter a bakery or a home with a roast cooking or if you smell ripe fruit heating on its tree in the sun. These flavors and aromas can be extracted manually for culinary use, and although their yield is small, it is concentrated. To be of any practical culinary use, we need to capture these tiny molecules and stabilize them before they vaporize, and to do this we provide them with a bulky carrier, in this case, oil. When you use the bulk carrier of boiling water, the end result is called tea, tisane, or herbal infusion. Because plant oils are to be used for aetherolea, it is useful to have some knowledge of their different characteristics, flavors, viscosities, and longevity.

OILS AIN'T JUST OILS ....
It's just a matter of time before the molecular structure of all foods breaks down, and oil is no different. You will know when it begins to happen by the increasing rancidity due to free radical forma-tion. The oil in some prepackaged nuts is often already rancid, making them bitter, and, for the sake of your health, you should always return them to the point of sale or throw them out. The life of your oil is affected by the following:

1. In general, the less refined the oil, the more flavor and color it has because of the suspended plant matter, but this also shortens its longevity. The more refined the oil, the longer its shelf life, but the less color and flavor it has.

2. Different oils also rapidly break down and degrade at dif-ferent temperatures, and this is called their "smoke point." It is the temperature at which your oil begins to discolor,

burn, and turn bitter, and when it chemically breaks down and decomposes. This varies slightly depending on many factors, including processing. Smoke point degrees should be seen as good approximations only. Because you will not be cooking your aetherolea, knowledge of each oil's individual smoke point is not essential, but it is useful to have a general idea. A summary of oil smoke points is included at the end of this book.

3. Oil oxidizes when exposed to air, and plant-flavored oils oxidize quicker depending on the type and amount of plant matter suspended. This process can grow a bacteria called "clostridium botulinum," which can lead to botulism; therefore, infused oil extracts should be stored no longer than twelve weeks, in a closed bottle or container, in dry, dark, and cool conditions. In a cupboard is fine, or the fridge, but you will need to rewarm oils to room temperature to regain liquidity. I advise making your flavored oil as you need it for maximum flavor and freshness.

4. Because all oils are sensitive to light, which causes them to lose nutrients and to oxidize, it's best to keep them in the dark. This is also why you will find the better quality and fruitier oils sold in dark glass and metal containers.

TECHNIQUE ....

To achieve edible aetherolea or a truly ethereal oil using the mortar and pestle, you simply pound and grind your chosen plant matter in the mortar, drizzle oil in slowly, and grind both patiently together with the pestle. This is food alchemy, where two become one; it's not a marathon, so you can let your mix sit a few times, coming back to taste and regrind occasionally. When the oil is the color and flavor intensity you prefer, it must then be strained well through a fine sieve or muslin, one or more times, until the oil is clean, transparent, and without sediment or particles. Chefs often use pipettes to drop infused oils onto finished plates of food. We keep ours in the fridge in small, long-nozzle, capped plastic bottles that can be squeezed to release a thin stream or a few drops at a time. Your chemist, art supplier, or kitchen shop may have these. Try looking for small travel packs and food grade plastics.

My general ratio for making aetherolea is four parts plant material to one part oil: e.g., for every 4 cups of fresh herb or plant material, you will need 1 cup of oil to carry the extract. Because a little goes a long way, start experimenting with ¼ cup oil to 1 cup herbs or plant material. The ratio can be varied as needed, e.g., when using highly pungent items like chilies, you may chose to use less plant matter, whereas for delicate flavors and colors such as violet or tarragon, you might like to try using less and more colorless oils.

Mint and eucalyptus oil extracts are both good to rub on sore joints or the temples for headaches, but eucalyptus oil is toxic if taken internally whereas mint oil is edible. So be sure to keep to domesticated edible plants, because it is in the kitchen that you will be using your oil extracts.

USES AND TYPES ....

Whether you are a professional chef or a novice cook, these bursts of intense flavor and splashes of bright, vibrant color will take your finished dishes to a whole new level of enjoyment. Aetherolea are primarily meant as an edible garnish, so always serve and plate your prepared food before you drizzle or add individual drops of your extract. How you use the oil and how much you use will depend on the type you've made, your palate, and your visual creativity.

Aetherolea oil use is, to a large extent, unexplored territory in the culinary world and an exciting area for the new chef or true pioneering spirit. You are limited only by your imagination, so experiment, be brave, and most of all enjoy the magical alchemy of the creation of new oil essences with the mortar and pestle. Examining the flavor and scent of the plant or herb with your eyes closed may give you some new ideas on pairing unlikely or unusual foods together. For example, sweet basil has a clove scent that pairs well with desserts made with fruit, egg, milk, or cream, so you could use walnut or macadamia oil for the carrier medium to give a further subtle, nutty depth. Thai or holy basil, sometimes called tulsi, has a clove flavor, as does Italian basil. Lemon and lime basil add citrus flavor, African blue tastes of camphor, and licorice basil of aniseed.

Try inventing your own heavenly oils and uses for them, or try some of our suggestions below.

- Drops of bright green basil or chive oil on creamy, soft yellow corn chowder.
- Beautiful white fish surrounded by alternate drops of green lime oil, yellow lemon oil, and red chili oil.
- Roast or grilled meat with pomegranate oil.
- Chocolate desserts with green mint oil.
- Soft white rice topped with a little Indian or Thai curry surrounded with chili-cardamom spots.
- Salad of rocket, fennel, and orange drizzled with dill oil.
- Prawns drizzled in sizzling garlic oil.
- Elegant pasta served surrounded with the colors of Italy: a pristine white glazed plate, with bright green basil and vibrant red tomato oil drizzles and/or drops.

— Garlic ground with sherry vinegar (or balsamic vinegar) and walnut oil used as a dipping oil.
— Bruschette topped with Parma ham, pear slices, and goat's cheese, drizzled with walnuts ground into walnut oil and a few drops of maple syrup.
— Walnuts ground with walnut oil, a few drops of dry sherry, and fresh cream, served with poached salmon or chicken breast.
— The amber color of macadamia oil enhanced to a burnished copper, pink or scarlet with pomegranate and/or honey and/or maple syrup, drizzled with cracked macadamia nuts and garnet pomegranate avrils to offset the silky white sheen of panna cotta or crème desserts.

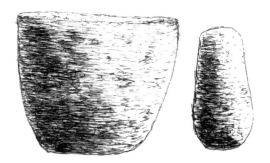

THE FAMILY OF EDIBLE OILS ....

Oil is a pure or purified fat of plant origin and is usually liquid at room temperature, with the exception that the more saturated the fat, the more solid it will be at room temperature (e.g., coconut and palm oils are saturated fats and generally only liquid in the tropics). Saturated fats are unhealthy and increase blood cholesterol, whereas monounsaturated and polyunsaturated fats are healthier alternatives and help reduce blood cholesterol levels. Trans fats also increase blood cholesterol and should be avoided. The type of oil you use for aetherolea is entirely up to you, the flavors you prefer, or the effect you are trying to achieve. You can choose from strong oils such as first-press olive or flaxseed, all the way through to the bland, pure, tasteless oils such as rice bran.

In 2008 the world consumed approximately 120 million tons of edible oils, and over the next forty years this amount is expected to more than double. For this reason, oil sources are continually being expanded to meet the growing demand of the market. For the choice of oil, therefore, we have included many edible oils that may not be familiar to you or are not currently widely available, but each has something unique to offer in its own right. As the old TV ads used to say, "Oils ain't just oils," so it can be fun to choose your domestic culinary oils with care and consideration.

Choose your edible oils from the following, depending on the application, the result you require, and your green conscience.

ALMOND ....

Also known as sweet oil in recipes; however, sweet almond oil comes from dry pressing the kernel of white-blossom almond trees, whereas bitter almond oil comes from dry pressing the kernel of pink-blossom almond trees. Almonds, which are technically not a nut but a fruit, have been popular since the times of the ancient Greeks and Persians. "Almond" is from the Latin "amandola," derived from the Greek "amygdala," and just as the walnut resembles the brain, the almond resembles this inner brain structure. Domesticated as early as the Bronze Age, the almond was one of the foods found in the tomb of Tutankhamen, dating from 2000-3000 BC, and is the state tree of India. Almond oil is light and viscous, usually clear, and makes an excellent carrier for sweet flavors and delicate colors.

ARGAN ....

The traditional oil of Moroccan Berbers, the nut of the argan tree is manually cracked, and its three kernels, looking like sliced almonds, are extracted, roasted, and stone ground. The cold pressed oil is darker than olive oil and has an unusual, robust, nutty flavor. It is one of the rarest oils in the world and a Moroccan delicacy used as a sweet drizzling oil or with vegetables. The argan tree, a relative of the olive, is native to and found almost exclusively in southwestern Morocco and is a relic plant species from the Tertiary age, over 1.6 million years ago. It is endangered and, since 1999, has been under World Heritage List protection by UNESCO, the United Nations Educational, Scientific, and Cultural Organization. Berber women have used the mortar and pestle for argan oil extraction for hundreds of years. All argan oil is produced by a woman's cooperative, and profits go to the women of the Berber tribe for health care and education. Each argan tree yields approximately thirty-two kilograms of fruit per season, the manual cracking of which takes several days. Two and a half kilo of kernels result in one liter of oil. At $200 a liter argan oil is now used as a substitute for truffle oil.

AVOCADO ....

One of the few oils extracted from the fleshy pulp rather than the kernel or seed of the fruit (along with palm oil). It has the highest smoke point of the edible oils at 520°F/270°C. This would usually

mean a good oil for frying; however, this is not the case, as avocado oil turns bitter when heated. It has a pale, delicate, green-
yellow color and a sweet flavor and is an excellent carrier of both
sweet and salty flavors.

CANOLA ....
A cultivar bred from rapeseed in the 1970s by two Canadian scientists, canola (its name standing for Canadian oil, low acid) is now
the most-produced oil seed crop in the world and recently was the
third largest crop produced by both Canada and Australia. It is
one of Monsanto Corporation's controversial Big Four genetically
modified crops along with soy, corn, and cotton. It is very cheap
and plentiful, a pale yellow in color, with high viscosity and a mild
flavor. It is highly refined, and its omega-3 fatty acids are generally damaged in the process. We find the aroma unpleasant, and
choose not to use this oil.

COTTONSEED ....
Cheaper even than canola, cottonseed oil is the refined, bleached,
and deodorized oil extracted from the seeds of the cotton plant.
Its flavor is mild, its liquid clear and light gold in color, but at 26
percent saturated fat, it is unpopular with nutritionists. Its long
shelf life makes it resistant to rancidity, and its high smoke point
of 450°F/230°C makes it a favorite with potato and corn chip
manufacturers, margarine and shortening producers. Because it
is cheap, hydrogenated cottonseed oil is used instead of butterfat
in many frozen desserts and ice creams, as a cocoa butter substitute, and is popular with salad dressing and mayonnaise manufacturers. It is genetically modified, and some studies have shown it
can cause infertility in rodents. We choose not to use this oil.

COCONUT ....
Oil is extracted from the kernel of the coconut palm and, as a satu-rated fat, it is generally liquid only in tropical temperatures. It is pungent with the smell of coconut, clear and viscous when warm, and opaque and white when not. For this reason it is seen by most chefs as unsuitable in the kitchen.

CORN ....
Extracted from the germ of the corn kernel, the oil is expeller pressed and solvent extracted, treated with alkali, refined, and deodorized. Invented in 1898 in Indiana, it was originally called mazoil. It is cheap and has a high smoke point, making it a cheap frying choice, used primarily as a fast-food cooking oil, and in the manufacture of margarine, soaps, paint, ink, and insecticides. It is one of Monsanto's Big Four genetically modified crops. It is high in omega-6 fatty acids and not recommended by nutritionists. We choose not to use this oil.

COLZA ....
A French specialty, it is closely allied with rapeseed oil and is used as a fine oil substitute especially with carpaccio and beef Bourguignon. It is also popular in Belgium, the United States of America, Germany, and the Netherlands. Colza oil is extracted from the seeds of the cross between the cabbage and turnip known as the swede. Also called rutabaga or yellow turnip, it was crushed commercially in China in the time of Chi Min Yaoshu for everyday use and was used in the United Kingdom and Europe before gas-lights for lighting streets, trains, and lighthouses. The oil is bright yellow and odorless.

FLAXSEED ....
Also called linseed oil. Little used in the kitchen today, it has a strong flavor. Used in paints, putty, and wood finishing, and, when combined with wood and cork dust and particles in 1860, it became known as the fabulous linoleum. Flaxseed oil, as the name suggests, is extracted from cold pressing the dried ripe seeds of the flax plant. Its disadvantages are its short shelf life, strong flavor, and rancidity without refrigeration. Its advantages are its high omega-3 content, nutritional supplement advantages, and its clear, yellow color.

GRAPE SEED ....
Prior to the twentieth century, the grape seed was discarded as a by-product of wine production until the United States and Europe began chemically extracting the oil. With 65 percent-72 percent linoleic acid, antioxidant properties, and a high smoke point of 421°-485°F, 216°C, grape seed oil became an instant hit. It emulsifies well and resists separation, making it attractive to commercial producers of mayonnaise and sauces. It has a fine texture, is odorless, light, and pale green in color. It assimilates the flavor of other foods well, is polyunsaturated, and is often used as a substitute for olive oil. Most commercial grapes are sprayed with chemicals, and unfortunately this concentrates in the seed and, therefore, the oil when it is refined. We use grape seed oil only from an organic source.

HAZELNUT ....
Pressed from the nut kernel of the hazelwood tree, the oil is also called cob nut or filbert oil. Turkey is the largest producer. Along with macadamia and walnut oils, hazelnut oil is very popular in modern Australian cuisine. It has a smoke point of 410°F/210°C

and a long shelf life and has replaced mink oil in cosmetics. Used in confectionary, pralines, truffles, and chocolates, it has a light-yellow, translucent color, and its slight nutty flavor can be enhanced further in the mortar and pestle by grinding it with fresh hazelnuts and sweet basil.

MACADAMIA NUT ....
Expressed from the nut meat of the large round nuts of the macadamia tree, this native to Australia has oil of a light amber, almost translucent color and is popular in salads. Ground with herbs, garlic, chilies, and fruit, it is an excellent carrier of both sweet and savory flavors, and with pomegranate and a few drops of honey or maple syrup, its amber color can be enhanced.

MARULA ....
The extracted oil of the marula tree is better known in South Africa, Mozambique, Namibia, and Natal than the West. The Bushmen and Bantu tribes use it as a preservative, as it can extend the life of meat for up to a year. The oil is clear, light yellow, and has a nutty aroma.

MONGONGO NUT ....
Also called manketti, this is a native of South Africa, hand collected, and cold pressed by hand by Kalahari Natural Oils (KNO). The oil is used by the Body Shop and the three thousand collectors' income has doubled recently from $100US to an average of $200US per annum.

MUSTARD SEED ....
The oil pressed from mustard seeds is hot, strong, and nutty, with a strong pungent aroma reminiscent of wasabi or horseradish.

Used primarily in India and Bangladesh, it can be extracted from black, brown, or white mustard seeds. It has 6 percent omega-3 and 15 percent omega-6 content.

OLIVE ....
It will come as no surprise that Mediterranean people use the most olive oil annually per capita but who would have guessed that Australians are their nearest rivals? Olive oil can be stored for years, but the extra virgin ones for only nine months, and flavored oil for twelve weeks. This is healthy oil for everyday use and has multiple applications with flavor that ranges from rich and pungent to mild and colors from grass green to pale blond, depending on the amount of filtering and processing.

PALM ....
Palm oil is extracted from the pulp of the fruit of the oil palm, and palm kernel oil from its seed. Palm oil has a reddish color due to its high beta-carotene content. Originally from western African countries, it has now expanded into Southeast Asia and has the lowest production cost of all major oils, making it an attractive export crop. Since 2006, Malaysia has the world's largest oil palm plantation. Whilst it is free of cholesterol itself, because it is a saturated fat that solidifies at room temperature, it increases the body's production of cholesterol. Its low cost makes it the base for some cheaper brand soaps and an everyday cooking oil in tropical Africa and Southeast Asia. Palm oil is high in nutrients, is mono-unsaturated, and, in its reddish form, adds natural color to fried foods such as potato. The red oil is refined, bleached, and deodorized for domestic use. A processing by-product is glycerin and also biofuel for transport, and its 44.3 percent palmitic acid content

was used, combined with naphtha, in World War II to produce napalm. A lot of people choose to avoid palm oil because of its negative environmental consequences, which include mass clearing and destruction of rainforest habitats in south-east Asia. We choose not to use this oil.

PEANUT ....

This pale yellow oil of the peanut is also called groundnut oil and is used primarily in Chinese, South Asian, and Southeast Asian cuisines. Because of its nutty flavor and high smoke point, it is ideal for wok or deep frying; however, like its parent, it cannot be used for those who are allergic to peanuts. The oil is generally extracted by pressing steam-cooked peanuts. This is also a crop that suffers from high chemical spray usage, so pay a little more and try and source organic unrefined peanut oil.

PECAN OIL ....

Extracted from the nut, pecan oil has a smoke point of 470°F/245°C, is very low in saturated fat at 7 percent, and has a slightly pecan but mainly neutral flavor.

PERILLA OIL ....

Also called the Asian beefsteak plant. Found mainly in China, the oil is pressed from the seeds of this annual herb of the mint family. It is used to flavor soups and stews and to fry cakes. Perilla oil dries to a hard yellow and is used in varnishes, paint, and medicines. It is high in omega-3 and has a lovely, bright green color with a delightful fragrance.

PINE NUT OIL ....

Also called pine seed or cedar nut oil, it is extracted from the edible seeds of various pine species. Because it has a low smoke point, it is not used to cook with but is perfect for finishing flavor. Prior to the revolution in Russia in 1917, it is estimated that 10 percent of all hard currency in the Russian economy was based on pine nut oil, which was traded primarily to France. It has appetite-suppressant properties and is used in China and Russia to aid peptic ulcers and gastritis.

PISTACHIO OIL ....

This cold pressed oil from the nuts of the pistachio plant has a strong flavor. Because of this, it does not blend with everything, but we think it matches well with sweet and salty foods. When blended with balsamic vinegar, it goes well with avocado, apples, pears, and grilled fish.

POMEGRANATE SEED OIL ....

It takes five hundred kilograms of fresh pomegranate fruit to collect enough seeds to extract one liter of oil. It tends, therefore, to be rare and expensive. However, it is worth the wait when you find it, and a little goes a long way. Pomegranate seed oil is high in lipids and pucinic acid, omega-5, and conjugated linoleic acid, and is therefore a powerful antioxidant and free-radical fighter. You can save the seeds from a pomegranate if you juice it and crush them in your pestle and mortar for a few drops of magic.

POPPY SEED OIL ....

Poppy seeds are small, kidney-shaped, slate blue seeds harvested from the walnut-size, ripened, dried seed capsules of the oriental or opium poppy, *Papaver somniferum* or *Papaver orientale*. This is the same frilly, flowered plant from which we get morphine, opium, and heroin; however, the seeds themselves are not narcotic. In 1400 BC Crete, poppy seed oil was used as a sedative, in 800 BC Homer grew the plants in his garden, and the ancient Egyptians mixed poppy seed oil with honey for temple confection offerings. In Afghanistan in 650 BC, cave paintings were made using poppy seed oil in the paint, in the Middle Ages it was popular as a spread for bread, and more recently iodized poppy seed oil was used medically as a carrier of radioactive dye agents in radiological identification of tumors and cancers.

PUMPKIN ....

Oil is extracted from the roasted, hulled seeds of the Stryian oil pumpkin. This light or dark, opaque, and generally thick oil has been used in Southeast Austria in Styria since 1697 and since the eighteenth century in Eastern Slovenia, Croatia, and Hungary. Pumpkin oil has an intense, nutty flavor of its own and can be ground with herbs or citrus and used with fish or vegetables. In a thin layer, it appears green, and in thicker layers, red. It can be added to dressings, desserts, or ice cream and, when added to yogurt, turns bright green-gold. It is high in lysine, but when cooked it turns bitter.

RAPESEED ....
The English word "rape" derives from the Latin "rapum," meaning "turnip." Although rapeseed oil has been used for hundreds
of years in Asia and India in oil lamps and as a lubricant in steam
engines, the first commercially available, edible rapeseed oil was
released in 1956-57. The Chinese and Indian cuisines seem to use
it most. It has a higher uric acid content than its cultivar offspring,
canola. Color is clear and the flavor mild.

RICE BRAN ....
Although the germ or embryo of rice is only 8 percent paddy
weight, it is 75 percent oil! Rice bran oil extracted from this inner
part of the rice grain is a relative newcomer to the oil market,
being invented and commercialized in 1994 in the United States
of America. It is seen as a healthy, nutraceutical oil. Rice bran oil
has a subtle, clean, almost nutlike flavor with high viscosity and a
color that varies from clear to cloudy. It is free of trans-fatty acids,
stable without hydrogenation, high in vitamin E, and has antioxidant properties. With its high smoke point, 490°F/254°C, it is
excellent for frying delicate flavors and popular for Japanese tem-
pura. It makes an excellent carrier for subtle flavors and colors.

SAFFLOWER ....
This thistlelike annual has multiple flower heads each carrying
fifteen to twenty seeds similar to sunflowers. Safflower petals,
seeds, and oil are one of our oldest domesticated foods. As far
back as the Twelfth Dynasty in ancient Egypt, textiles were dyed
with safflower, yellow from the petals, and red, carthamin from
the seeds, and its importance was such that a garland of safflower
was found sealed in King Tutankhamen's tomb in the Valley of the

Kings. Safflower oil has been used in India, the United States, and Mexico since the nineteenth century. The color is pale yellow. It has the second highest smoke point at 510°F/265°C.

SESAME ....

Also called till or gingelly oil, this is extracted from the ripe seed capsules of the sesame plant. An old and revered oil, sesame was used in ancient Syria around 600 BC in food, as a salve (see "Unguents"), and in medicine (applied topically for treating a wide range of ills, from anxiety, depression, and insomnia to headache, joint, and back pain). The Sanskrit and Hindi words for "oil" derive from the word for "sesame," and it was seen as sacred and used in Hindu and Buddhist temples to light votive lamps. The smell of burning sesame oil is thought in some religions to be preferred by the gods and the spirits of the dead. High in vitamins E and K, it is used in Southern Indian, Korean, and Chinese cooking and ranges in color from pale yellow to dark brown, depending on whether it is cold pressed from raw seed or hot pressed from roasted seed. It has 41 percent omega-6 polyunsaturated fatty acids, a long shelf life/high smoke point, and is high in antioxidants. In 1943 a mutant strain of sesame plant was developed to avoid the seed shattering and thereby try and increase the yield of seed crops; however, there still remains today a worldwide shortage of this pungent and most delicious of ancient oils. Try grinding with pink salt and pink peppercorns and add a few drops to soup or bruschetta. For a mega sesame hit, grind some sesame oil into some sesame seed paste or water-hulled tahini and spread on steak or toast with fresh mango or white peach flesh.

SOYBEAN ....
This cheap, highly processed, genetically modified vegetable oil accounts for more than half the world's edible vegetable oil production. Its 16 percent saturated fat and 51 percent oxidation-prone linolenic acid should make it undesirable as a commercial cooking oil, but it is widely used. To extract the oil, the soybeans are cracked, the moisture content adjusted, and the soybeans heated to between 140°F/40°C and 190°F/70°C. Then they are rolled and the oil solvent-extracted with hexane. (Hexane is refined from crude oil, smells like gasoline, of which it is a significant constituent, and is used in shoe glues and many degreasers.) The extracted soy oil is then refined, blended, and sometimes hydrogenated.

SUNFLOWER ....
This nonvolatile oil comes from the seeds of sunflowers. Low in both saturated and trans fats, it has between 48 percent and 74 percent linoleic acid and is high in vitamin E. It has a clear, amber color and a clean, somewhat fatty taste and aroma. Kettle, Walkers, and Lays fry their potato chips in sunflower oil rather than the cheaper oils.

WALNUT ....
This delicate, light topaz-colored and floral-scented specialty oil is extracted from the walnut kernel from the fruit of black walnut trees and is our personal favorite. Walnut oil is clean, light, nutty, and rich in omega-3, coenzyme Q10, vitamins E and K, and lecithin. In traditional oil extraction in Perigord and Burgundy, France, nuts are crushed with giant granite grinders, the homogenous mass then roasted and pressed while still warm, and one

liter of oil extracted from six kilograms of nuts, resulting in a mild, delicate, and subtle flavor. Australia, New Zealand, and California are also walnut meat and oil producers. Beware the cheap imitation walnut oils on the market, where a cheaper oil is infused with macerated walnut meat, adding almost no flavor at all, or the overfiltered, too-pale varieties. The traditional and best walnut oil is made from large roasted nut pieces and has a short shelf life, and for this reason is often sold in tins. It lasts between six and twelve months once opened, which is never a problem in our kitchens.

WATERMELON ....

Also called Kalahari oil or Ootanga oil, the oil extracted from the seeds of watermelon is used primarily in the Kalahari Desert in West Africa. The oil is cold pressed from the dried seeds and was used in ancient Egypt five thousand years ago. High in omega-6, it also has zinc and iron. This oil is wonderfully light and fragrant.

PLANT INFUSERS ....

The herbs and plant foods that you can use to infuse your oil are endless. See *The Culinary Library* volume on edible flowers and leaves for additional ideas. Or try some of the following, either singly or in multiples: basil, beetroot, cardamom, caraway, chives, celery, citrus, chervil, chili, chocolate, clove, coriander, dill, fennel, garlic, ginger, juniper, lavender, lemongrass, mint, mustard, nuts, paprika, parsley, peppercorns, pomegranate, rose, rosemary, sage, tarragon, thyme., violet.

LOTIONS, POTIONS, AND ELIXIRS

———•◆•———

"There is but one genuine love-potion – consideration"
—MENANDER OF ATHENS, 342-292 BC

It is not possible to replicate the original recipes for all of the following because some are either lost in time or fiercely guarded secrets. Others, though, have been handed down in one form or another through centuries of use. You might experiment using your mortar and pestle occasionally for some interesting lotions, potions, and elixirs.

BENEDICTINE ....
Bruise in the mortar 1 tablespoon each of cardamom seeds, myrrh, and mace, and 1 teaspoon each of galangal root, ginger, and orange peel. Add to 175 ml alcohol and 75ml water. Steep 1 week, strain, and add to it the following: 17 grams caramel, 235 ml spirit of nitrous ether, 1 ml solution of ammonia, 15 grams vanilla sugar, 8 grams licorice juice, 28 grams acetic ether, 1.5 grams coumarin, 2 gram each oils of lemon and bitter orange, 15 drops oil of anise, 12 drops oil of bitter almond, 7 drops oil of sassafras, 4 drops oil of hyssop, 2 drops each oils of hops and cardamom, 1gram oil of galangal, 40 drops oil of wormwood, 15 drops each oils of ginger and cascarilla, 10 drops oil of millefoil, 6 drops oil of angelica, 1 drop each oils of juniper and rosemary. Increase the amount to

500-530 milliliters by adding drinking alcohol. Steep for 2 weeks before straining. Add sugar syrup to taste and the same volume again in alcohol. Age as required.

BITTERS ....

A recipe for a simple amaro or bitters.

Bruise the following in the mortar and then steep in a bottle of alcohol for 2 weeks. Vodka is fine. Strain and add sugar syrup to taste, then age as required.

5 leaves lemon balm
5 leaves sage
10 leaves rosemary
10 leaves wormwood
15 juniper berries
5   cloves
1   piece each of cinnamon, orrisroot, calamus root, gentian root
$\frac{2}{3}$ cup water

SCOTTISH BITTERS ....

In Scotland these bitters are traditionally drunk before meals purely to aid digestion and for good health.

In the mortar, bruise the following, then steep in a bottle of whiskey for 2 weeks. Strain, add sugar syrup to taste, and age as required.

30 gram gentian root, 15 grams coriander seed, 7 grams bitter orange peel, 4 grams chamomile flowers, 7 grams whole cloves, 7 grams cinnamon stick.

CHARTREUSE ....

Green Chartreuse:

Bruise in the mortar 1 gram star anise, 10 grams coriander, 1 gram sage leaves, 1 gram melissa leaves, 1 gram mint leaves, 1 gram angelica leaves, 10 grams tansy, 0.5 gram saffron. Steep in 1 liter of alcohol for 2 weeks. Strain. Add sugar syrup made from 700 grams sugar/2 liters water. Age as required.

Yellow Chartreuse:

Bruise in a mortar 4.5 grams saffron, 1.5 grams cinnamon, 4 grams coriander, 6 grams melissa, 6 grams fresh hyssop stems and leaves, 3 grams angelica. Steep in 1 liter of alcohol for 2 weeks. Strain. Add sugar syrup made from 300 grams sugar/1 liter water. Age as required.

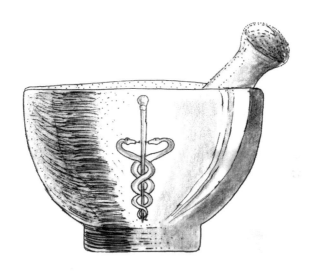

COLD AND FLU POTION ....

Flesh only of 1 lemon
2 green peppercorns
2 tablespoons honey
2 tablespoons glycerin
2 tablespoons brandy or cognac

DANDRUFF LOTION ....

Inspired by the 1550 BC Ebers Papyrus.
Lightly toast equal parts barley and bran in a pan, then grind together in the mortar and pestle and add fish oil to make a smooth paste. (The ancient Egyptians suggest that sour fermenting wheat can also be used, as can hippopotamus oil if you have a supply handy.)

ELIXIR OF YOUTH ....

An old recipe inspired by the 1550 BC Ebers Papyrus.
Grind fenugreek seeds in your mortar into a powder and mix with water to make a soft paste. Apply to the face to remove wrinkles and blemishes and to beautify the skin. Grind and mix equal parts of honey, Epsom salts, and alabaster grains. Use in the same way.

GOLDEN SILK ELIXIR ....

Take the hairy silk from a fresh corn cob and grind with 1 tablespoon honey and a little lemon juice. Stir into 1 cup of boiling water. Cool slightly and sip to aid gallstones, rheumatism, and incontinence.

INSTANT LIMONCELLO

2 tablespoons sugar
2 lemons, zest or shaved skin
Grind in a little boiling water, just enough to dissolve the sugar.
2 tablespoons lemon juice
Vodka to taste
Chill. Sip from small glass neat or mixed with soda and ice.

LIVER CLEANSER ELIXIR

Grind 1 tablespoon grated carrot and 1 tablespoon grated apple with 1 tablespoon citrus peel, 1 tablespoon diced tomato pieces 1 tablespoon green tea. Place into a 2-cup teapot and fill with boiling water. Steep for 3-5 minutes. Pour through a strainer and sip.

LOVE POTION 1

To attract true love:
3 small pink rose hearts
3 teaspoons honey
3 teaspoons brandy

LOVE POTION 2

To attract attention:
3 lovage flowers or leaves
1 teaspoon lemon peel
1 teaspoon honey
1 teaspoon lemon juice
¼ teaspoon cinnamon
5 tablespoons vodka

MIRACLE SKIN LOTION ....

1,000 international units vitamin E tablets plus 25,000 international units vitamin A tablets
1 tablespoon almond oil
1 tablespoon avocado oil
1 tablespoon olive oil
1 tablespoon sesame oil
(Can pierce and empty gel caps for vitamins if you do not have tablets.)

ROSE LOTION ....

Grind 1 cup of fresh rose petals with 2 tablespoons bran. Add ¼ ripe avocado, 1 egg yolk, and 1 tablespoon cream or yogurt. Apply to dry, flaky skin on face, neck, hands, and arms. Wash off after 20-30 minutes.

SALVATION ELIXIR ....

Also known as Elixir Salutis or Daffy's Elixir in 1649. Used to banish despair and regain hope.
1 teaspoon licorice root
1 teaspoon senna pod
1 teaspoon aniseed
1 teaspoon jalap
1 teaspoon rhubarb
1 teaspoon elecampane root, optional
1 teaspoon raisins
½ teaspoon fennel seed
½ teaspoon parsley seed
1 drop cochineal
1 cup brandy
Grind dry ingredients, add wet ingredients, then steep for 15 days. Strain, then take 1 teaspoon of the liquid 3 times a day.

SHOW WU CHINESE ENERGY TONIC ....

1 tablespoon root of *Polygonum multiflorum*

1 tablespoon root of *Angelica sinensis*

1 tablespoon root of *Polygonatum sibiricum*

1 teaspoon root of *Rehmannia glutinosa*

1 teaspoon root of *Ligusticum wallichii* (Chinese lovage)

½ teaspoon cardamom seed

1 clove

VITAL LIFE ELIXIR ....

2 tablespoons grated fresh horseradish

2 tablespoons grated fresh onion

2 tablespoons grated fresh ginger

2 garlic cloves

4 tablespoons cider vinegar

1 cup boiling water

After grinding, keep in a plastic or glass container in the fridge and have 1 teaspoon morning and night.

.

POULTICES

"Patience is a Poultice for all wounds"
—PROVERB

A poultice is a moist, soft mass, usually made of plant material that is spread on a warm or hot cloth and traditionally applied topically to the skin to reduce inflammation, pain, and disease. The poultice is sometimes referred to as a drawing salve and can also include clay and sometimes pharmaceutical medication. "Poultice" is from the Latin word "puls" or "pultes" and means "porridge." Another word used to describe poultices is cataplasms.

Poultices were traditionally made from bread or cereal. In all cases, only material known to be safe should be applied.

The heat of the poultice relaxes the pores of the skin and opens them, allowing the innate healing properties of the vegetable matter to enter and draw out puss and inflammation. The smell of the poultice can noticeably deteriorate over the thirty minutes or so it is used. This may simply be a sign that it is drawing puss and inflammation from the pores. Plant poultice is thrown away after use and is never used on open wounds. You can wrap the poultice matter in a large cloth handkerchief, gauze, or clean cotton or muslin cloth. You can also make or buy small cloth or gauze bags, turn them inside out at the end of use to shake out the plant matter, and then put them into your normal wash cycle. To apply the poultice, heat a piece of cloth or bag in hot water and squeeze. Cover with and fold or insert the plant matter mixture. Place over the affected area for approximately thirty minutes. You will need to cover with plastic wrap to hold in place if you are moving about. Remember, poultices are old home remedies invented before modern medicine, they do not replace medical treatment so always consult your doctor before use.

BRAN POULTICE ....
Mix bran with hot water and apply for 30 minutes to the affected area for bruises, strains, sprains, and inflammation.

BREAD POULTICE ....
Grind some stale bread and moisten with milk; put into hot cloth and use for boils, abscesses, and to draw out slivers, splinters, or shards of glass or wood.

CABBAGE POULTICE ....

Grind raw or cooked cabbage with a few sprigs of basil and moisten with a little boiling water. Leave on for 30 minutes for ulcers, varicose veins, shingles, dry and itchy skin, gout, rheumatism, burns, and cramps. Use for 10 minutes only over the liver area to detoxify. For red and itchy skin, add 1 teaspoon Epsom salts to the grind.

CARROT POULTICE ....

Parboil or grate the quantity of carrot required and grind with a little vegetable oil to moisten for use with cold sores, cysts, boils, and skin infections.

CLAY POULTICE ....

Any clean, powdered clay mixed with a little cider vinegar and water, when applied as a warm poultice, has been used to assist skin inflammations, bruises, and acne.

GREEN TEA POULTICE ....

Green tea leaves or matcha powder moistened with or soaked in boiling water, when applied to the skin, can assist with blackheads, ingrown hair follicles, acne, sagging skin, and dull skin.

JACK AND JILL POULTICE ....

Fist published in the early 1700s, the nursery rhyme "Jack and Jill" has several versions, but all agree it was a vinegar and brown paper poultice that was used.

Jack and Jill went up the hill to fetch a pail of water,

Jack fell down and broke his crown and Jill came tumbling after.

Up Jack got, and home did trot,
As fast as he could caper,
He went to bed to mend his head
With vinegar and brown paper.

Crush a good cup of whole fresh sage leaves in the mortar, then add boiling vinegar to just cover. Steep 3–5 minutes, then remove the softened leaves and lay them on a double thickness of clean brown paper. Fold paper into a flat package, folding the ends in to seal, then place over bruised, painful, swollen, or strained areas. Cover with a towel to retain heat. Leave until totally cool and the swelling and pain will subside.

MUSTARD POULTICE ....

Grind ½ cup mustard seed with ½ cup flour and hot water, then place in hot cloth and wrap with plastic film for 10-30 minutes to ease coughs (neck), colds, flu (chest), arthritis, and asthma. Porridge mixed with mustard and applied to the chest in Victorian times was called a mustard plaster.

ONION POULTICE ....

Mix parboiled or grated or finely chopped onion with a little flour and hot water to treat inflammation and to reduce scarring.

Add 1 tablespoon mustard powder and some mint leaves to treat headache and sinus infection (put on forehead or hold plaster behind the ears for infection), and over the lower abdomen for bladder infection.

POMEGRANATE POULTICE ....

Pound and grind pieces of pomegranate skin with some leaves, if you have them, and moisten with boiling water. Apply to aid dry skin, relieve itching, and drive out bad luck.

POTATO POULTICE ....
Mix parboiled or grated potato with a little flour and boiling water to sooth arthritis, boils, and carbuncles.
Grated raw potato ground with black peppercorns in a warm poultice, placed on the forehead for 1 hour, can help a migraine headache.

PLANTAIN POULTICE ....
Pound to a mash a plantain, moisten with boiling water or oil, and apply for burns, scrapes, and insect bites.

PUMPKIN POULTICE ....
Poultices of ground pumpkin flesh and seeds were reportedly used by the American Indians for drawing puss and inflammation.

WALNUT POULTICE ....
Grind and pound walnuts with their skins and moisten with fish oil or cod liver oil. Greater benefit occurs, if you have access to growing walnuts, if you grind the whole nut, including its shell, while it is still soft and green. Used to treat headache and dry, sagging skin.

UNGUENTS

"For faith and love prepare oil and unguents."
—HIPPOLYTUS OF ROME 204 AD

"Unguent" is a word our grandmothers or mothers might remember but today is no longer used. "Unguent" is an English translation of the Latin "unguentum," from the root "ungere," which means "to anoint." Unguents, therefore, mean "ointments" or "salves." They were once also called "pomatum," from the Latin "pomum," meaning "apple," which was one of the ingredients macerated into grease to make an ointment. "Unguent" generally refers to a soothing preparation that is spread on the skin to aid burns, wounds, rashes, abrasions, and itches. Think ointment, but oilier and less viscous; a semisolid paste, a salve, or a balm. Unguents are salves for soothing or healing.

Since ancient times, unguents have been made from fats or greases like rendered animal lard, beeswax, or olive oil with soothing or healing active ingredients incorporated. In both the ancient world and the Middle Ages, they played an important role in medical treatment. Examples still available from chemists and health food stores include arnica for bruises, balsam, carron oil for burns, lip balms, mentholated salves like Deep Heat, zinc ointment, lanoline, and chrism or sacramental oil, which is a mixture of oil and balsam.

In the Middle Ages, unguents were seen as a form of witchcraft or devil's work. Owning a copy of *Des Science Occultes*, by Eusebe Salverte, written in 1829, was a sure way to get tied to a tree stacked with kindling, anointed in rendered pig fat, and set alight for the purification of your soul. Thankfully we are more liberal and educated now, but there are still people today who think that mixing your own potions, lotions, unguents, and elixirs is living on the edge of what is considered normal. Some preparations are contraindicated for pregnant women or persons who suffer from high blood pressure, insomnia, or mental illness. Please check with your medical professionals to ascertain your individual circumstances.

Modern unguents or salves are made by mixing warm beeswax (available at most health food stores) with oil that has been infused with the essential oils and properties extracted from plant materials. The beeswax will be sold in a solid form and can be warmed gently prior to grinding. Most of the following recipes use fresh plant material and are intended for use before the plant matter deteriorates. If you have sensitive skin, please ensure you do a patch test before applying to delicate areas. As these are old home remedies, please seek medical advice for any medical conditions and do not ingest.

ALTHEA ....
Also known as marshmallow salve or ointment, althea is made from grinding the roots, flowers, seeds, or leaves of the marshmallow plant into a wax base. The resulting salve has been used since ancient Egyptian times for sore throats, wounds, chest coughs, sunburn, skin eruptions, and blisters. It also has cleaning properties and was used as a hair treatment and Persian rug restorer.

APOSTLES' UNGUENT ....
Several sources reference an unguent in use prior to 1700 AD made up of twelve ingredients said to represent each of the twelve Apostles of Jesus. Its use was to "cleanse foul sores." There are no surviving recipes, but it may have been similar to Apostolicon, an unguent containing olive oil and litharge of lead (lead oxide) or a simpler version of the "regale ungentum" or "royal unguent" of the ancient Parthian kings, whom the Roman scholar Pliny the Elder

wrote about in the first century CE. Parthia later became part of Persia, and was formerly Assyria. The full "royal unguent" was thought to be red because of the use of henna, but it also contained a number of other spices and herbs, including ben (myrobalan), patchouli, cinnamon, cardamom, spikenard, zatar, myrrh, cassia, gum storax, ladanum, balsam, calamus, ginger grass, thorny trefoil, galbanum, saffron, nut grass, marjoram, cloves, honey, and wine.

BALM OF GILEAD ....

Populus balsamifera, the European black poplar tree, has resin in both the bark and buds (the buds of Gilead), which were thought to have healing properties for inflammation and rheumatism. By mixing with beeswax, this resin makes a light green-yellow unguent with a fragrant balsam/lavender smell. Also known as Populeum.

BASILICUM ....

Basil is thought to have originated in Egypt, and certainly its use as an antiseptic salve seems to have originated in the ancient world. To crushed leaves and stalks, grind in some beeswax, olive oil, and a few drops of oil of turpentine. Use externally to draw out stings, bites, and poisons from the skin. Also used for joint pain.

BLACK DRAWING SALVE ....

2 tablespoons softened beeswax, 3 tablespoons cocoa butter, 3 tablespoons shea butter, 2 tablespoons of organic coconut oil, 1 tablespoon vitamin E oil, 2 tablespoons activated charcoal powder, 3 tablespoons bentonite clay, 5 drops essential oil of lavender.

Traditionally applied to boils, stings, splinters, eruptions, or any skin that needs poison or foreign bodies to be drawn out.

BLACK WALNUT SALVE ....
Probably the most useful of all the general salves to keep on hand. Grind and pound the pithy, outer green husks of two unripe walnuts and add to this 2 tablespoons olive oil and 2 tablespoons beeswax. If you want a smoother, creamier salve, you can also add 1 tablespoon honey or 2 tablespoons cocoa butter or 2 tablespoons shea butter; however, these are optional. Black walnut salve is traditionally used to assist blisters due to heat or fever, itching, rash, dry or inflamed skin, and athlete's foot.

CAMPHORIUM ....
As the name suggests, this salve was used as a decongestant and rubbed onto the chest. There is no surviving recipe for camphorium from the Middle Ages, but beeswax with added camphor would be a good start, perhaps then adding a few drops of the soothing essence of lavender, lemon, sage, or eucalyptus.

CHEST CONGESTION SALVE ....
1 tablespoon beeswax, 1 tablespoon wintergreen, 3 tablespoons olive oil, 3 tablespoons eucalyptus oil, 3 tablespoons camphor oil. You can add fresh mint if it is available.

COLD CREAM ....
Also known as white unguent, the best known album is cold cream, which was invented around 129 AD by the prominent

Roman physician Aelius Galenus or Claudius Galenus, who was better known as Galen of Pergamon. Although originally of Greek birth, Galen was physician to five Roman emperors, and his white *unguentium* is still made today and sold as cold cream. In the mortar and pestle, mix 4 tablespoons of sweet almond oil or olive oil and 1 tablespoon melted beeswax together. Stir a pinch of borax into a small cup of rosewater and add very slowly to the oil/wax mixture, emulsifying and blending as you do so with the pestle. Just before the mixture refuses to absorb any more liquid, add a few drops of organic cider vinegar and rose absolute if you want a stronger perfume. Let it cool in the mortar, and then transfer to a clean jar. Once used as a night cream to rejuvinate the face.

EUCALYPTUS SALVE ....
2 teaspoons elder oil, 2 tablespoons beeswax, 2 teaspoons eucalyptus oil, 2 teaspoons wintergreen oil. For joint pain and inflammation.

FLYING OINTMENT OR SEER SALVE ....
The unguent with the greatest longevity down through the centuries would probably be flying ointment. An early variation of it was probably used in ancient Egypt by temple priests to aid in visions when communicating with the gods. The recipe that has survived from the Middle Ages is, as far as can be determined, as follows:

In any order mix and grind 3 grams each of lavender, passionflower, wormwood, hops, poppy petals, skullcap, and dittany of Crete.

To this add 3 drops each of jasmine, rose otto, and matricaria chamomile.

To this add 9 drops each of juniper berry oil, bog myrtle oil, yarrow oil, and Mysore sandalwood oil.

To this add ¼ cup wheat germ oil, ⅔ cup jojoba oil, and 1 cup of melted beeswax. (If beeswax is unavailable you can substitute almond oil, but it will not be an unguent consistency.) Store in fridge. Used topically only, on wrist, inside elbows, temple

GOMBAULT'S CAUSTIC BALSAM ....
This was a famous French veterinarian recipe popular as a horse and human liniment in the late 1800s and for obvious reasons is no longer used.
60 milliliters cottonseed oil
15 milliliters croton oil
4 milliliters camphor oil
2 milliliters turpentine oil
15 milliliters kerosene
1.25 grams sulphuric acid

HOLY ANOINTING OIL OR UNGUENT ....
The New King James Bible, Exodus 30:22-30, has the following to say: "Moreover the Lord spoke to Moses, saying: 'Also take for yourself quality spices—five hundred shekels of liquid myrrh, half as much sweet-smelling cinnamon and of sweet-smelling cane, five hundred shekels of cassia, according to the shekel of the sanctuary, and a hin of olive oil. And you shall make from these a holy anointing oil, an ointment compounded according to the art of the perfumer. With it you shall anoint the tabernacle of meeting and the ark of the Testimony; the table

and all its utensils, the lampstand and its utensils, and the altar of incense; the altar of burnt offering with all its utensils, and the laver and its base. You shall consecrate them, that they may be most holy; whatever touches them must be holy. And you shall anoint Aaron and his sons, and consecrate them, that they may minister to me as priests.' " An ancient shekel was approximately 28 grams, and the ancient hin was approximately 3.5 liters. So to make the holy salve or anointing unguent in the mortar and pestle, grind approximately 1 tablespoon of liquid myrrh, 1 tablespoon of cassia, ½ tablespoon cinnamon, and ½ tablespoon sugar into 1 cup of liquid beeswax. Use olive oil if you want a liquid.

HONEY BALM ....

This all-purpose antiseptic balm is easy to make in the mortar and pestle. Mix into a few spoonfuls of warmed beeswax some almond oil, tea tree oil, lavender oil, and honey.

INSOMNIA SALVE ....

1 tablespoon each of rosemary, mint, calendula, sage, lavender, and olive oil. When thoroughly ground and mixed, add 2 or more tablespoons beeswax. Apply to both temples 1 hour prior to sleep. Used to help induce relaxation and sleep. May also induce vivid dreams.

LIP BALM 1 ....

4 tablespoons extra virgin olive oil
4 tablespoons softened beeswax
Squeezed contents of 4 vitamin E capsules

LIP BALM 2 ....
4 tablespoons shea butter, 3 tablespoons jojoba oil, 2 tablespoons extra virgin olive oil, 4 tablespoons softened beeswax.
To add flavor to lip balms, add a few drops of essential oils, such as peppermint, spearmint, vanilla, cinnamon, lavender, or ginger, or add in your favorite crushable lolly (hard candy).

MEDEA SALVE ....
Myth has it Prometheus taught Medea how to make this salve from mandrake root, and she made it for Jason to give him strength and protection in his quest for the Golden Fleece. It was made by grinding fresh mandrake root to a paste with grape seed oil, extra virgin olive oil and melted beeswax.

POMATUM ....
Although the name "pomatum" suggests apple, unguent pomatum was originally made from pig fat. It can be replicated today by mixing rosewater and lemon essence into warmed beeswax. It can be used as a skin and hair conditioner and softener.

POPULEON ....
Also called the balm of Gilead, populeon was popular in the 1400s in Europe. Extract the resin from European black poplar buds in the mortar by crushing, and grind the resin into softened beeswax. In the past this was used for gout, inflammation, and bruises.

SAGE AND VIOLET SALVE ....
For lips, cold sores, and chapped skin.
2 tablespoons chopped sage leaf, 2 tablespoons violet flowers, 4 tablespoons almond oil, 4 tablespoons softened beeswax.

ST. JOHN'S WORT SALVE ....

2 tablespoons St. John's wort leaves, 1 tablespoon each of calendula, comfrey leaf, plantain, and olive oil. When ground together,
add 2 or more tablespoons of beeswax. Used topically on the skin
for skin irritation, minor burns, itching, and rash.

MISCELLANY

*"Poor indeed is the garden in which
birds find no homes."*
—ABRAM L URBAN

FURRY and FEATHERED FRIENDS:

ANIMAL HOOF OIL ....
An excellent hoof oil for dry, hard, cracked, or chipped hoofs can
be made in the mortar and pestle. Simply mix 1 teaspoon gum
turpentine, 1 teaspoon cod liver oil, 2 teaspoons thick lanoline,
and 4 teaspoons neat's-foot oil. (Make double if your set is large
enough.) Apply to the hoof, coronet, and frog daily for improve-
ment, then weekly for maintenance.

PET CRUMBLE ....
For variety, break down your cat's or dog's pelleted dry food with
the pestle and add some grated cheese, a raw egg, and a tablespoon of omega-3 or walnut oil.

WILD BIRD FEEDER 1 ....
The mortar is the perfect shape to make a hanging bird feeder.
Fill your mortar ½ or ¼ full with wild bird seed mix (in the pet-
food aisle in your supermarket).

Melt 100-200 grams drippings or lard (next to the butter in your supermarket) in a small saucepan and pour over the seeds mix until just covered.

If you want to hang it later, insert a knotted string or fine wire hook to the bottom, in the middle. To help it stand, loop the longer, free end midway around a chopstick or the handle of a wooden spoon and rest it across the mortar. Refrigerate until it sets. Sit in a bowl or sink or kettle of hot water for a few minutes to melt the outer edge to lift out easily.

Hang in a tree or place on a bird saucer or feeder.

WILD BIRD FEEDER 2 ....

This is a good pantry clean-out exercise. Pound together any or all of the following items you have kept too long in your cupboards:

Raisins and currants (robins and thrushes)

Dried apples, dates, prunes, sultanas (all birds)

Peanut butter (sparrows and wrens)

Bread products (wrens, sparrows, robins, blackbirds)

Molasses, honey, treacle, golden syrup, sugars, oatmeal, cereals, crackers, flour, seeds, nuts. Cover with melted drippings or lard.

An alternative to inserting a hanging hook is to refrigerate the mixture, and, when set enough to spread, scoop the mixture out with the tip of a knife or a small spoon and pack into open pine cones. These can be wired onto tree branches or hung in a sheltered spot.

Wild bird feeders are especially important in the cold winter months because birds cannot store enough fat, and many struggle to find food. They are also useful in sustaining adult birds in spring when they are busy feeding their chicks before themselves.

CANINEFELINE ICE BLOCKS ....

Grind a whole ripe banana in the mortar with a cup of rolled oats or any breakfast cereal. Add 2 tablespoons peanut butter and 1 tablespoon omega-3 oil. Spoon into a few ice cube trays or a couple of cupcake cups, depending on the size of your cat or dog. You can add some milk if you want it to go further. Freeze as a treat for your pet to lick outside on a hot day.

CANINEFELINE TREATS ....

1 garlic clove
½ cup grated cheese
½ cup bran flakes
2 tablespoons oil

Pound all together, roll into small balls, and keep in a plastic container in the fridge.

TRAVELERS' TRANSLATIONS OF MORTAR AND PESTLE

Can there be anything more enjoyable, in any city of the world, than coming across, unexpectedly, an Aladdin's cave of culinary delights? Only the knowledge, perhaps, that with that first, inevitable step over the threshold, you will find not only some new and wondrous discoveries but perhaps an exciting acquisition to take home, use, and admire. Just in case you are about to head off on an exotic trip up the Nile, into darkest Africa, to the exotic Far East, or perhaps just down to your local Chinatown precinct, We have included some translations. Just photocopy the page and take it with you so you can make the most of any culinary markets, bazaars, or shops. Aladdin escaped his cave with an old lamp; perhaps you will return home with the ancient mortar and pestle.

Arabic: هقدملاو نواهلا عفادمب
Albanian: Llaç dhe shtyp
Chinese: 砂浆和杵
English: Mortar and Pestle
Danish: Mortel og Pestle
Dutch: Mortier en Stamper
French: Mortier et Pilon
German: Mörser und Stößel
Greek: Ιγδίο
Italian: Mortaio e Pestello
Japanese: 臼と杵
Lebanese: Jom and Modaqqa
Malay: Lumpang and Lesung
Russian: Ступку с пестиком
Serbian: Bacac i Mrviti Tuckom
Spanish: El Mortero y maja en Mortero
Swedish: Mortel och Pestle
Turkish: Havan topu ve Havanda
Vietnamese: Vữa và đâm bằng chày

SMOKE POINTS OF OILS

APPROXIMATE SMOKE POINTS OF OILS IN ASCENDING ORDER BY TEMPERATURE

200°F/93°C and up:
Canola oil, unrefined
Flaxseed oil, unrefined
Sunflower oil, unrefined

300°F/149°C and up:
Corn oil, unrefined
High-oleic sunflower oil, unrefined
Olive oil, unrefined
Peanut oil, unrefined
Safflower oil, semi-refined

375°F/190°C is the normal temperature for deep frying:
Soy oil, unrefined
Walnut oil, unrefined
Coconut oil
Sesame oil, unrefined
Soy oil, semi-refined
Olive oil, semi-refined
Macadamia nut oil
Corn oil

400°F/205°C and up:
Canola oil, refined
Walnut oil, semi-refined
Olive oil, extra virgin
Sesame oil
Cottonseed oil
Grape seed oil
Olive oil, virgin
Almond oil
Hazelnut oil
Canola oil
Rapeseed oil
Peanut oil

Sunflower oil
Corn oil, refined
High-oleic sunflower oil, refined
Peanut oil, refined
Safflower oil, refined
Sesame oil, semi-refined
Soy oil, refined
Sunflower oil, semi-refined
Olive oil, extra light

500°F/260°C and up:
Safflower oil
Avocado oil, refined

NB: 600°F/315°C is the flash point of oil when it catches fire. The smoke point of an oil decreases with each repeated heating, with contamination by salt or food particles, exposure to light and oxygen, and as it thickens and darkens.

APPROXIMATE SMOKE POINTS OF OILS BY ALPHABETIC ORDER

Almond oil: 430°F/220°C
Avocado oil, refined: 520°F/270°C
Butter: 350°F/175°C
Canola oil, unrefined: 225°F/107°C
Canola oil, semi-refined: 350°F/175°C
Canola oil, refined: 400°F/205°C
Coconut oil: 350°F/175°C
Corn oil, unrefined: 320°F/160°C
Corn oil, refined: 450°F/232°C

Cottonseed oil: 420°F/215°C
Flaxseed oil, unrefined: 225°F/107°C
Hazelnut oil: 430°F/220°C
Grape seed oil: 420°F/215°C
Lard: 361°-401°F/183°-/205°C
Macadamia nut oil: 389°F/198°C
Olive oil, unrefined: 320°F/160°C
Olive oil, extra virgin: 406°F/208°C
Olive oil, virgin: 420°F/215°C
Olive oil, extra light: 468°F/242°C
Peanut oil, unrefined: 320°F/160°C
Peanut oil, refined: 440°F/227°C
Rapeseed oil: 438°F/225°C
Safflower oil, unrefined: 225°F/107°C
Safflower oil, semi-refined: 320° F/160°C
Safflower oil, refined: 510°F/265°C
Sesame oil, unrefined: 350°F/175°C
Sesame oil, semi-refined: 450°F/232°C
Soybean oil, unrefined: 320°F/160°C
Soybean oil, semi-refined: 350°F/175°C
Soybean oil, refined: 450°F/232°C
Sunflower oil, semi-refined: 440°F/227°C
Sunflower oil, unrefined: 225°F/107°C
Sunflower oil, refined: 450°F/232°C
Walnut oil, unrefined: 320°F/160°C
Walnut oil, semi-refined: 400°F/205°C

MORTAR & PESTLE

NOTES

2819322R00084

Made in the USA
San Bernardino, CA
07 June 2013